MW00634561

Chappaquiddick
Tragedy

Chappaquiddick
Tragedy
Kennedy's
Second Passenger
Revealed

Donald Frederick Nelson

PELICAN PUBLISHING COMPANY
GRETNA 2016

The word "Pelican" and the depiction of a pelican are trademarks of Pelican Publishing Company, Inc., and are registered in the U.S. Patent and Trademark Office.

Library of Congress Cataloging-in-Publication Data

Nelson, D. F. (Donald Frederick), 1930- author.
    Chappaquiddick tragedy : Kennedy's second passenger revealed / Donald Frederick Nelson.
        pages cm
    Includes bibliographical references and index.
    ISBN 978-1-4556-2114-9 (hardcover : alk. paper) — ISBN 978-1-4556-2115-6 (e-book) 1. Kennedy, Edward M. (Edward Moore), 1932-2009. 2. Kopechne, Mary Jo, 1941-1969. 3. Keough, Rosemary 4. Traffic accidents—Massachusetts—Chappaquiddick Island. 5. Chappaquiddick Island (Mass.)—History. I. Title.
    E840.8.K35N45 2015
    973.92092—dc23
    [B]
                                    2015026651

Printed in the United States of America

Published by Pelican Publishing Company, Inc.
1000 Burmaster Street, Gretna, Louisiana 70053

Contents

Preface

Several decades have passed since Edward M. Kennedy's Oldsmobile Delmont 88 careened off Dike Bridge on Chappaquiddick Island in 1969, killing Mary Jo Kopechne. Can anything new be said about the mysteries left behind by the cover-up surrounding that wreck? After you read this account, I think you will answer, "Yes!" And what you will read is based solidly on recorded facts of the time that are all cited in the notes at the end of this book. This is not a work of imagination or conspiracy theories.

When all legal action against Kennedy ended and the inquest testimony was released, the *New York Times* editorialized, "'The case is closed,' says the Dukes County District Attorney. So it is in a legal sense; but it is not resolved." And that unresolved case involved a prominent U.S. senator and had national political repercussions. It was, in fact, the most famous automobile accident of the twentieth century! Clarity, understanding, and resolution are needed. Historical truth demands them.

How has Chappaquiddick defied resolution? Several factors have served to entangle people's thinking about the cover-up. First is confusion about what was being covered up. After all, Kennedy admitted to being the driver who left the scene of a fatal accident, so what was left for him to cover-up? Had he done something worse? Imagination and conspiracy theories quickly took charge of some people's thinking. Then, political leanings entered to produce sympathy or antipathy, prejudicing the viewpoint and detracting from objective evaluation of known evidence. Misplaced trust in some participants' accounts also led to acceptance when skepticism was needed. Finally, the abysmally inadequate police investigation and prosecutorial questioning at the inquest produced no resolution to the Chappaquiddick case.

How have I avoided these pitfalls? It all started with a rumor I heard long ago about a third person in Kennedy's car. It was interesting because it accounted for some of the peculiarities of the case, but it was just a rumor. Later I chanced upon a Bill Kurtis presentation of *Investigative Reports: Chappaquiddick* on A&E and was fascinated to see how the forensic evidence he presented was consistent with that scenario. After Kennedy died, when I felt I would not be accused of political motives one way or the other, I decided to explore the Chappaquiddick documents, press coverage, and earlier analyses from the viewpoint of that story. It directed me to pose different questions, be skeptical of previous interpretations, and reject the conspiracies and pure imaginings of some previous writers. As supporting information accumulated, I realized in steps that I wasn't exploring a "rumor" or "scenario" or "story" but was discovering the true account of the Chappaquiddick accident and how the participants handled it.

This account can, must, and does stand on its reason, facts, and citations. In spite of the many previous examinations of this accident, I have found an unanalyzed piece of evidence, an ignored interview, a never-understood inquest testimony, and an uninterpreted participant statement, each unappreciated or unexplored before now, that serve as keys to unlock the mysteries of the cover-up. When you finish this book, I think you will say, "That makes sense! That pulls the cover off the cover-up. That solves the Chappaquiddick case."

Acknowledgments

The many reinvestigations of the Chappaquiddick accident, such as those by the *Boston Globe* in 1974 and the *New York Times* in 1980, have added to the original records. So have the authors of previous books, particularly Leo Damore, with his investigative reporting and interviews with participants in *Senatorial Privilege: The Chappaquiddick Cover-up,* a book still worth reading. Bill Kurtis's *Investigative Reports: Chappaquiddick* broadcast on A&E and available on DVD presented useful forensic evidence and interviews. These contributions have become a part of the historical records that I have built upon, and I wish to acknowledge their importance to this work.

I also want to thank Leslie H. Leland, foreman of the grand jury; John N. Farrar, the Edgartown Fire Department water-rescue expert; and Howie Hall, a crewman on Kennedy's boat, *Victura,* in the regatta, for their interviews with me. Their clarifications are described in the text and cited in the notes. In addition, I wish to thank Nicholas Lamar Soutter for his support of this writing project.

Lastly I want to thank my wife, Mickie, for her patience throughout my researching and writing of this book.

Chappaquiddick
Tragedy

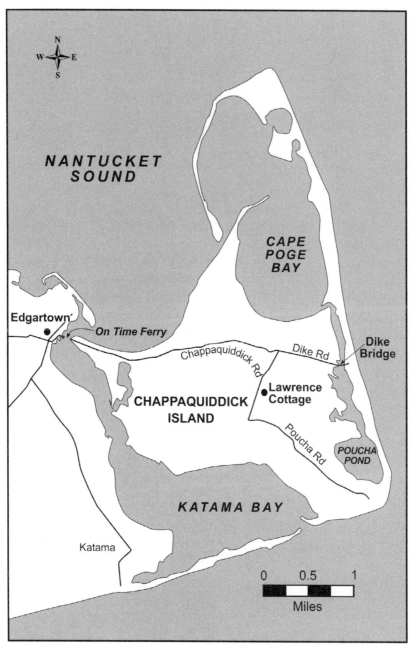

Map of Chappaquiddick Island (Mapping Solutions)

Chapter 1

The Party

It was to be a fun weekend with competitive sailing, partying with a group of close friends, and relaxing away from the pressure cooker of Washington politics. It was the weekend of the annual Edgartown Yacht Club Regatta on Martha's Vineyard Island and, with the Senate going into a three-day recess, a perfect July weekend for Edward "Ted" Kennedy to throw a party. He would be sailing in the regatta with his close cousin Joseph A. Gargan, as he had for many years. The party was to be a reprise of a much-appreciated party held a year earlier for the six young, single women whose intense involvement in Robert F. Kennedy's presidential campaign had left them grief-stricken following his assassination on June 5, 1968.

The six had worked in Bobby Kennedy's tense and confidential campaign "boiler room," where convention delegate support was counted and monitored. It was the nerve center of the campaign, and its committed staff shared an esprit de corps. After the assassination, the six had remained bonded, perhaps even more strongly so, and Ted felt he should lend continuing support to his brother's devoted staff through a friendly, relaxed getaway. Ted needed it too, for he had been the most keenly affected of all, having then lost two brothers to assassination. The 1968 party was a small but important event during the ten weeks that Ted spent out of the national spotlight recovering from shock, overcoming sadness, and evaluating his new identity as the Kennedy standard bearer. That sailing weekend with old friends had been helpful, return-to-normal therapy for all of them.

For the reprise party planned to begin on Friday, July 18, 1969, Joe Gargan leased a secluded cottage on Chappaquiddick, a part of Edgartown but at the time a separate island from the rest of Martha's Vineyard. Usually a sandbar, called Norton Point Beach, encloses Katama Bay on the south and connects Chappaquiddick to South Beach of Martha's Vineyard, but a storm had breached it then (and did again in the spring of 2007). Thus, Chappaquiddick was accessible at the time only by the *On Time* ferry, a simple motorized platform that held two vehicles as well as pedestrian traffic and crossed the narrow channel entrance to Edgartown's inner harbor in a little over three minutes.

Due to its isolation, Chappaquiddick had a year-round population at the time of only twelve in its six square miles of low, rolling, sandy hills covered with pitch pine, scrub oak, and vines. Although in the summer the population rose to some four hundred, it remained a quiet, remote

The On Time *ferry approaching the Chappaquiddick landing* (Associated Press)

place of scattered and hidden homes with no store, inn, restaurant, gas station, or church. It was a good place for a private party.

In the weeks before the regatta, many were invited for the weekend gathering, but other commitments led several of them to decline. As the late July weekend approached, only twelve were expected to attend. These included the six soon-to-be-dubbed "boiler-room girls" — Rosemary "Cricket" Keough, twenty-three; Susan Tannenbaum, twenty-four; Esther Newburgh, twenty-six; Ann "Nance" Lyons, twenty-six; her sister Maryellen Lyons, twenty-seven; and Mary Jo Kopechne, twenty-eight. Also expected were Paul F. Markham, thirty-nine, a former U.S. attorney of Massachusetts; Charles C. Tretter, thirty, a Boston lawyer and Kennedy campaign worker; Raymond S. LaRosa, forty-one, a Federal Civil Defense official stationed in Massachusetts and a stalwart Kennedy campaign worker; John B. "Jack" Crimmins, sixty-three, an investigator in the Suffolk County district attorney's office and longtime evening and weekend chauffeur for Ted Kennedy when he was in Massachusetts; and, of course, Kennedy and Gargan. Ted's wife, Joan, was expecting a baby and could not attend. The wives of the other men (except Crimmins, who was a bachelor) did not join them either.

None of those who crowded into that small Chappaquiddick cottage that Friday evening could have imagined the looming tragedy that would soon take the life of one of them, disrupt all their lives, and affect Kennedy's political fortunes for the rest of his life.

It is worth remembering that at that time Ted Kennedy was the heir to the formidable Kennedy political legacy following the tragic loss of his older brothers, Pres. John F. Kennedy, assassinated in Dallas in 1963, and Sen. Robert F. Kennedy, assassinated in Los Angeles in 1968 while seeking the Democratic nomination for president (not to mention his eldest brother, Joseph Kennedy, Jr., a navy pilot, killed in World War II). John Kennedy's Massachusetts Senate seat, vacated when he assumed the presidency in January 1961, had been carefully filled until the next congressional election by the appointment of a man with no further political ambitions. This allowed Ted Kennedy, who had just turned thirty, the constitutionally mandated minimum age of a senator, to run for the Senate in 1962 to fill out the last two years of his brother's term.

Ted had little to run on besides the family name, but he was the most naturally political of the Kennedy brothers and had a congenial personality. Ted was tall and well built, with a shock of dark wavy hair, a handsome, youthful face, and a ready smile and handshake. That was enough to defeat his accomplished opponent, State Attorney General Edward J. McCormick, Jr., in the Democratic primary and then to defeat the Republican nominee in the special fall election, George Cabot Lodge, scion of a politically prominent Boston family. When Ted ran for a full term two years later, he garnered 72 percent of the vote in a runaway victory. Ted took naturally to the collegiality of the Senate and became popular among his colleagues. As the Democratic Party Convention in Chicago neared in 1968, a spontaneous "draft-Teddy" movement sprung up to prevent Hubert Humphrey from getting the Democratic Party nomination for president. Kennedy vacillated, still in turmoil over Bobby's death and unsure that he was ready for the presidency. At the last minute he backed out, issuing a statement that he would not accept the nomination. But by the beginning of 1969 he had regained his footing and, as the new Congress convened, challenged Russell Long for assistant majority leader, or "whip," and won. The cover story of the next issue of *Time* magazine featured Kennedy and spoke of his "lustrous presidential prospects." Many at that time regarded him as a shoo-in as Democratic nominee for president in 1972.

The Chappaquiddick cottage was a modest, one-story, weathered-grey shingle house with yellow shutters. Facing but set back from Chappaquiddick Road (the north-south section that was sometimes called School or Schoolhouse Road), it was owned by Sidney Lawrence of Scarsdale, New York. Its main room was a long, narrow, living-room-dining-room combination with a fireplace, separated from the adjacent kitchen by a waist-high counter, which served as the bar for the party. The cottage had just two small bedrooms, each with twin beds, and a single bathroom. It was not intended to be living accommodations for the group. Apart from Crimmins and Markham, no one planned to stay there; it was to be just the party site. The boiler-room girls were put up

Sen. Edward M. Kennedy in 1969 (© Underwood & Underwood/CORBIS)

in three adjacent rooms at the Katama Shores Motor Inn (also called The Dunes, from its restaurant) in the sparsely developed grass plain extending to South Beach called Katama, about three miles south of Edgartown. Gargan, who as usual had done all of the planning for Kennedy for the weekend, had obtained rooms for the men at the Shiretown Inn on North Water Street in Edgartown.

Edgartown is a tony community characterized by 150-year-old, white clapboard-sided whaling captains' houses with black shutters and immaculate white picket fences. Even the more recent construction along the narrow, one-way streets emulates that style. Several posh inns and hotels offer the vacationer elegant accommodations, service, and dining. Art galleries, upscale apparel shops, and seafood restaurants abound. From Edgartown's center at the intersection of the east-west Main Street and the north-south Water Street, the Edgartown Yacht Club is one block eastward, the Shiretown Inn is two blocks northward, and the *On Time* ferry slip is three blocks northeastward.

The yacht club is now over a century old and has held "The Regatta" annually since 1924. Its many-windowed, weathered-shingle clubhouse is built on a pier jutting into Edgartown harbor. Its two-and-a-half-story main hall might be described as frugal Yankee style, but model ship hulls, sailing-race paintings, and nautical artifacts give it a sailor's decor. Both the Edgartown and Chappaquiddick sides of the harbor are dense with moorings for sailing yachts and powerboats, while a central traffic channel allows travel through to Katama Bay to the southeast. The regatta occurs to the north of the harbor

The Sidney Lawrence cottage used as the party site on Chappaquiddick (© Bettmann/CORBIS)

in Nantucket Sound. In 1969, over two hundred boats were entered in the fifteen racing classes of the regatta.

Crimmins was the first of the party to arrive, bringing Kennedy's 1967 black Oldsmobile 88 sedan to Martha's Vineyard on the Woods Hole-to-Vineyard Haven ferry on Wednesday, July 16. Crimmins was on a close, casual basis with the senator from his longtime chauffeuring and so was included in the Chappaquiddick party in spite of his lack of sophistication and frequently crude language. Gargan, Markham, and a third crew member, a young man named Howie Hall, sailed Ted's boat, *Victura*, a twenty-eight-foot, blue-hulled, Wianno Senior-class sloop, from Wianno, Cape Cod, to Edgartown harbor on Thursday afternoon. Raymond LaRosa arrived alone by ferry, driving his Mercury sedan, in late afternoon that day. That evening, Rosemary Keough, Mary Jo Kopechne, Susan Tannenbaum, Esther Newburgh, and Charles Tretter arrived as foot traffic at the Vineyard Haven ferry terminal, having been driven from Boston to Woods Hole by Tretter. Gargan met the group at the terminal and dropped Tretter at the Shiretown Inn, where he roomed with LaRosa, and the four boiler-room gals at the Katama Shores Motor Inn. The two Lyons sisters arrived by ferry from Woods Hole in midmorning on Friday and were also met by Gargan. Then, early Friday afternoon, Kennedy flew in from Washington to the Martha's Vineyard airport, was picked up by Crimmins, and was taken via the *On Time* ferry directly to the Chappaquiddick cottage.

After a quick change into his swimming trunks, Kennedy was driven back on Chappaquiddick Road to the intersection that was to become famous later that night. The road takes a sharp, banked, ninety-degree left turn westward there to reach the *On Time* ferry slip. But to join the swimming party at East Beach, Crimmins made a ninety-degree right turn eastward off the pavement onto the bumpy, sand-and-gravel Dike Road, which leads to Dike Bridge, slightly angled to the left. Dike Road ends at the wide sandbar that is East Beach, just beyond the then-primitive, wooden bridge and the 100-yard-long causeway maintained by post-and-plank revetments. The boiler-room gals were already there, sunning and swimming. With the first race scheduled for midafternoon, Kennedy had time only for a quick dip.

The intersection of the paved Chappaquiddick Road, turning left toward the ferry slip, and the sand-and-gravel Dike Road, beginning at the right and leading to Dike Bridge and East Beach (© Bettmann/CORBIS)

Dike Bridge takes its name from the dike that once extended completely across the narrow channel entrance of Poucha Pond and was built to give vehicle access to East Beach. Then in 1949, the dike was broken and the bridge constructed to allow tidal flushing of Poucha Pond from the larger, almost enclosed saltwater Cape Poge Bay to the north. Dike Bridge was given a pronounced hump in its middle to allow fishing boats to enter Poucha Pond.

After his short swim and another change of clothes at the cottage, Kennedy and the rest of the party headed to Edgartown for the first of the regatta's races, which the young women would watch from an arranged spectator boat. Kennedy rendezvoused with his boat near the ferry slip on Chappaquiddick, wading out to come aboard. The morning breezes had died, postponing the race start, and the near-calm persisted, making the race less than exciting. It was also disappointing because the Kennedy-captained *Victura* placed ninth in the Wianno Senior-class race, well behind the winning boat, *Bettawin*, captained by Kennedy's friend and racing rival Ross Richards. Invited to a victory party aboard the *Bettawin* at dock, Kennedy tossed down three rum-and-cokes while chatting with his friend Stan Moore, whose boat had placed third, before heading to the Shiretown Inn a short walk away to check in. It was then well past six o'clock. The second-floor room that he shared with Gargan was in Mayberry House, a separate building at the rear of the main Shiretown Inn. It had a deck with a flight of stairs down to ground level. The two of them entertained a few friends on the deck with a half-dozen Heinekens ordered from room service.

Shortly after seven o'clock, Crimmins drove Kennedy across to Chappaquiddick on the *On Time* ferry. They were the first ones of the group to arrive at the party cottage. As intended by his early arrival, Kennedy climbed into a bathtub of hot water to soak his aching, once-broken back after the exertion of the race, since his Shiretown Inn room had only a shower. Gargan, Markham, and Tretter soon arrived in a rented white Plymouth Valiant, which Gargan drove back to the ferry landing to pick up the others.

The central activity at the cookout was grilling steaks over an outdoor charcoal grill, overseen by Gargan. Of course, before the steaks were served, the group enjoyed an extended cocktail time with oven-heated hors d'oeuvres. With the evening hot and balmy, the partygoers spent almost as much time outside around the grill as inside the small, cramped, and un-air-conditioned cottage. They kidded Kennedy good-naturedly about his race result, reminisced with campaign stories, and generally filled the air with lighthearted chatter.

Crimmins had purchased and brought to the Vineyard a very large quantity of rum, vodka, scotch, and beer. Though all the participants at the party played down the amount of drinking in their inquest testimonies given six months later, it is clear that as the evening progressed, the party became rather raucous, with substantial drinking. Kennedy had a reputation for heavy drinking at times, so one can imagine he led the way. Gargan, in an interview many years later, said, "Some people at the party had had quite a few, no question. Frankly, everybody's a little bombed, except for Ray LaRosa."[1] As the drinking continued, the gaiety increased, the chatter grew louder, music from a radio blared, several couples danced, and everyone present boisterously sang old Irish songs.

The noise level 110 yards away at the home of Foster Silva became intolerable, keeping him awake in bed for an hour, until around 1:30

A.M. He recalled, "There was a lot of singing and laughing coming from the house. I would say it was a normal cocktail party. They were damned loud, though."[2] His son-in-law described it more graphically as "one of those loud, noisy brawls" with "yelling, music and general sounds of hell-raising."[3] Silva's wife, Dodie, remarked that night, "Boy, they must be having a heck of a time. I hope they don't wreck the place."[4] She said the loud noise continued until 1:30, causing her dog to bark continually and keep her awake.[5] Then the party quieted noticeably but continued until she fell asleep at 2:30. With the night hot, still, and muggy, all the cottage's windows were wide open, allowing even the interior noise to flow through the intervening woods. Later testimony indicated there was frequent traffic in and out of the cottage long after midnight.

Perhaps the best measure of how carried away the partygoers had become is that most of them had not planned to spend the night in the cottage, intending instead to take the *On Time* back to their booked rooms. The six young women and four of the men had brought no overnight bags to the cottage. Only Markham, who had given up his room at the Shiretown Inn to Kennedy, and Crimmins intended to sleep there. The others' failures to even attempt to catch the *On Time*'s last run, usually at midnight but available later on call for a premium, strongly suggest a collective, alcohol-induced, carefree gaiety.

With the traffic in and out of the cottage all evening and the commotion of twelve people in a small cottage (and perhaps impaired perception and memory after a number of drinks), it is not surprising that no one remembered, according to an interview with Esther Newburgh a few days later, when Kennedy left the party or with whom (until, that is, their prepared and rehearsed inquest testimony six months later).

What was about to happen — the most famous automobile accident of the century — would fill newspaper, magazine, and television reportage and opinion columns for the next ten months and lead to controversy, acrimony, and, for some, outrage for decades to come. How could a car crash cause so much interest and consternation for so long? Because everyone perceived a cover-up, a cover-up successful because of the fame, power, and influence of the driver: Ted Kennedy.

The account of the accident and its aftermath presented in the following chapters has not been told before.

Chapter 2

The Accident

In relating the happenings of this fateful night, I choose to accept observations and testimony from disinterested parties over the participants' likely self-protecting or friend-protecting testimony. Thus I assert that, in contradiction to Kennedy's later testimony, he left the party in his Olds 88 at close to 12:40 A.M., well after the customary last *On Time* run, with a female companion.

This is known from the testimony of Christopher "Huck" Look, a fuel-oil distributor and part-time deputy sheriff, who was on special duty at the Edgartown Yacht Club's Regatta Dance that Friday evening. Huck Look was a highly respected man with a character "as straight as an arrow." He would soon be appointed sheriff for an unexpired term in 1971 by Massachusetts governor Francis Sargent and then would win five successive elections to five-year terms.

Look's duties at the club that night ended at 12:30 A.M. He was taken on the club's launch across the harbor to the ferry slip on Chappaquiddick, where he picked up his parked car and headed for his summer residence. As he made the sharp, ninety-degree, southward turn of Chappaquiddick Road, a large, dark-colored car, coming from that direction, passed through his headlights, with a man driving and a woman in the front passenger seat. In his first remarks to the press, he said he saw two women in the car, the second in the backseat.[1] In his later comments and inquest testimony, he was less sure of his backseat observation, saying he saw something: a third person, an object, or perhaps only a shadow. As Look completed the sharp turn, he saw in his rearview mirror that the car proceeded straight through the intersection northward, off the asphalt paving onto the narrow, dirt Cemetery Road, and then stopped. Thinking the driver was confused or lost, Look pulled his car over to the side and got out to offer aid. As he approached the car, it suddenly went into reverse toward him, stopped abruptly, whipped around, and sped off eastward on the sand-and-gravel Dike Road.

Due to his police training, Look glanced at the license plate in the brief moment that the car was about twenty-five feet from him. It was a Massachusetts plate with the letter *L* followed by a series of numbers both beginning and ending with *7*. (Kennedy's car registration number was identified as *L78 207* the next morning. A later check by authorities of the other eight large cars with plates beginning with *L7* in Massachusetts found that none of those had been on Martha's Vineyard on that night.[2]) Look, of course, had no idea at the time how important this chance encounter was to be, though he did mention it to his wife upon arriving home.

Kennedy, undoubtedly wanting to avoid being recognized with a female companion and to avoid a possible sobriety check by a uniformed officer, roared off on Dike Road toward East Beach, throwing up a cloud of dust. His immediate reaction to flee from an officer was a repeat of his behavior in Virginia while in law school, for which he was convicted of "racing with an officer to avoid arrest"[3] (among several other traffic charges). Though he had been driven onto Dike Road and across and back over Dike Bridge on the previous afternoon, he approached the bridge at much too high a speed for the oblique left turn (twenty-seven degrees from straight ahead) onto it and, apparently, for his impaired reaction time. Kennedy testified at the inquest that his speed was only twenty miles per hour, but later expert analysis concluded it was closer to forty miles per hour.[4]

Dike Bridge at that time was a rather primitive single-lane, entirely wooden structure that was eighty-one feet in length and supported by pilings, spanning the tidal-channel inlet to Poucha Pond. The plank roadbed was bordered by a rub rail just four inches high by ten inches wide; there was no guard railing. Between the rub rails, the roadbed was just ten and a half feet wide.

Dike Bridge with Kennedy's Olds 88 partly retrieved from Poucha Pond (© Bettmann/CORBIS)

The tracks of Kennedy's car showed that it made no attempt whatsoever to turn onto the bridge, left ambiguous skid marks but clear gouges in the rub rail, and plunged straight off the right side of the bridge into Poucha Pond. As its right front wheel dropped off the bridge before the left front wheel did, the car began rotating in the air and hit the water flat on the passenger side, with sufficient force to crush the two doors on the right side a few inches inward and shatter their glass. The right-side front and rear fenders were severely dented also. Water is essentially incompressible, and its inertia prevents its immediate displacement. Thus the car bounced off the water, as a thrown, skipping flat stone does, continued to rotate, and landed on its top with sufficient force to produce a broad dent in the roof. That caused widespread cracking of the front windshield, which the safety-glass lamination held intact. It then sank to the bottom, upside down with the rear end elevated from a combination of the weight of the engine in front and a trapped air pocket in the trunk.

As the water rushed in around their heads, Kennedy and his companion were in a terrifying situation — upside down, sinking fast in over six feet of water, and trapped inside the automobile. The driver's-side window was already open for a breeze on the muggy night (the car had no air conditioning). Stunned, disoriented, and filled with fear of drowning, Kennedy nonetheless was able to grasp the windowsill and pull himself down and out through his window (the door was later found still locked). He was followed out by his female companion, who occupied the front passenger seat, either through her broken-out window or his open window. Struggling to the surface, they gasped for air and then, with an incoming tide and a few swim strokes, reached the eastern shore on the south side of the bridge. Exhausted and shocked by the traumatic experience, yet exhilarated by their survival with no significant injuries, they sat on the sandy bank recovering for a quarter-hour or so.

As they believed themselves to have been the only occupants of the car, there was nothing further to do and no need to ask for help from anyone. Specifically, they did not knock at the house nearest the bridge, known as Dyke House, leased for the summer by Sylvia Malm, her husband, Pierre, and their daughter, also Sylvia. The backdoor light was lit, and in the darkness, it could not have been missed, if needed. Neither did they stop at a cottage on the other side of Dike Road where a very visible children's front-bedroom light was left on. And Kennedy did not want to report the accident at that time, fearing a sobriety test and wishing that his attempted tryst not be revealed. Past those two lights, the blackness of the night was disorienting. The moon had set two and a half hours earlier, and with no city glow, the heavens were almost as black as the woods bordering the road. Only that slight difference allowed Kennedy and his companion to negotiate Dike Road back to its intersection with Chappaquiddick Road. After turning left, they had the surer footing of tarmac to guide them toward the Lawrence cottage. Also, the wider road reduced the tree covering, increasing visibility. They passed the volunteer firehouse about 150 yards before the cottage and across the road. Its outside, red light was burning above the always-unlocked door for access to its emergency alarm. But once again Kennedy passed by an opportunity to report the accident. The 1.2-mile walk from the bridge to the cottage took a half-hour or so.

Thus, Kennedy's arrival there, about 1:30 A.M., may account for the noticeable drop in party hilarity at that time heard by Dodie Silva in the neighboring home.

Who was the young woman who had accompanied Kennedy on this fateful late-night drive? She was one of the boiler-room gals, obviously, but which one? (It is well known, of course, that Kennedy identified his only companion as Mary Jo Kopechne, who did not survive the wreck, but let us not get ahead of the story.) Rosemary Keough is an immediate candidate, because her flowered, lunch-pail-shaped handbag containing cosmetics, toiletries, a wallet, and keys to her motel room was found resting on the ceiling below the front passenger seat in the overturned, submerged automobile. And Kennedy evidenced their familiarity by calling her "Cricket" the next morning. In contrast, in a police report that morning, Kennedy could only write *Miss Mary* for Mary Jo Kopechne, omitting the "Jo" she always used and saying he could not spell "Kopechne." Keough was, in fact, employed at the time by the Kennedy family's Children's Foundation, a three-month-old organization dedicated to helping mentally retarded children.[5] Mary Jo, however, had specifically told her mother that she did not want to work for Ted Kennedy.[6]

Keough, however, has maintained that she left her handbag in the car earlier in the evening, when she accompanied Tretter back to Edgartown to obtain a radio for the party. That is surprising, given that a young woman's purse is often regarded as inseparable from her as an appendage. And Keough would have to have forgotten it for close to three hours before Kennedy left in that car. Tretter could offer no confirming testimony that the handbag had been in the car on the trip or had been left there afterward.[7]

Neighbor Dodie Silva, in a published interview, offered observations that challenge whether Keough was even in the car with Tretter on this errand. Dodie said she saw a "middle-aged man with silver hair" drive past her house toward the ferry in a car, which she realized was Kennedy's the following morning when she saw it pulled from Poucha Pond.[8] She observed the car pass at around 9:00 P.M., approximately the time of Tretter's errand in search of a radio. Further, she said it was the same man and same car that drove by in the same direction earlier in the evening. Tretter had, in fact, gone on an earlier errand back to Edgartown about eight o'clock to get ice, tonic, and cigarettes for the party. Dodie, from her cottage property, viewed the right, or passenger's, side of the car and saw the driver distinctly enough to recognize him as the driver she saw an hour earlier. *She mentioned no passenger in the front seat that, if there, would have obscured her view of the driver, been immediately noticeable, and likely prevented such specific identification of the driver.* While Tretter's hair was not "silver" nor graying, one might suppose that a setting sun on the far side from Dodie's view gave it a silver lining, as clouds have from a similar perspective. However, the sun had set at 8:12 P.M. that evening, too early for such an explanation to be valid. Could Dodie have been thinking of seeing him pass on his first errand, when the sun could have produced the silver lining? One thing seems clear: Dodie's view of Tretter was clear enough for her to take note of his hair, which photographs from the time indicate was prominently bushy.

In spite of this published report, Dodie was not called to testify at the inquest held months later, and so this observation — and elaborations that questioning could have brought out — was not entered into the record. Instead, Keough's explanation was simply accepted at face value by Police Chief Dominick J. Arena on the morning following the accident and also by the prosecutor and judge during the inquest. There were no probing questions about the handbag's presence in the car, as there should have been.

Let us examine the "forgotten handbag" scenario more closely. First, if Keough's story is accepted, the handbag would have been left on the front seat. After all, why would she, or any young woman who thought her purse important enough to take on such an errand, toss it in the backseat? Now imagine that the handbag had been left on the front seat and that one of the boiler-room gals later climbed into that seat to go with Kennedy on the fateful ride. *Unless that young woman were the owner of the purse,* she would almost certainly have said something like, "Oh, here's Cricket's handbag. Let me take it in to her," and promptly returned it to Keough in the cottage. (This would be particularly true if

Charles C. Tretter, Boston attorney and Kennedy campaign worker (Steven Hansen/The Life Images Collection/Getty Images)

Kennedy and his companion were actually turning in for the night, as later claimed.) Only Keough, upon entering the car that evening, would have retained the handbag there. Thus the handbag's presence in the car at the time of the accident points to Kennedy's front-seat companion being the handbag's owner, Rosemary Keough, whether it had been left there earlier or not.

Recall also that the purse was found on the ceiling of the front-seat compartment of the overturned, submerged automobile. Imagine that the handbag was sitting on the front seat or the person's lap before the accident. As the car plunged from the bridge and rotated to the right, the handbag, after perhaps floating in air for a moment, would have been tossed against the companion, the front passenger door, or its imploding window as the car hit the water on its right side. As the car bounced and continued to rotate to an upside-down orientation, the handbag would have flown through the air, bounced off the front windshield when the car decelerated, and landed on the ceiling below the passenger seat. As the car began to sink, with the engine pulling the front end down first, water initially rushed in only through the two front-seat windows, one open and the other blown out, and then moments later through the one blown-out rear window. Thus much more water flowed into the front-seat compartment than into the backseat compartment. Any tendency to wash the handbag to a new location was toward the rear. But it was found in the front and so must have been in the front at the start, rather than starting in the rear and washing to the front. And as reasoned above, it must have been with its owner. Thus, careful thinking about the "forgotten handbag" scenario, never done following the accident, points to Rosemary Keough as Kennedy's front-seat companion when his car plunged off Dike Bridge.

Esther Newburgh, who was designated to speak for the group of young women in the days following the accident, apparently sensed from reporters' questions or possibly from her own knowledge that Keough needed an alibi. So Newburgh supplied one when asked, stating she "could not recall that Miss Keough ever left the party."[9] Six months later, at the inquest, Keough offered a diametrically opposite explanation of her movements: she testified she had taken two long walks away from

Rosemary Keough, one of the media-dubbed "boiler-room girls" (John Loengard/
The Life Picture Collection/Getty Images)

the cottage with Tretter from around midnight to 2:00 A.M., the crucial time period of the accident. However, Judge James A. Boyle of the District Court, after no probing questioning whatsoever on this issue, accepted Keough's account of leaving her purse in the car on the errand with Tretter as fully explaining its presence in the wreck.

Who is Rosemary Keough? Barely five feet tall, red-headed, and daughter of a well-to-do Philadelphia family, she graduated from Manhattanville College, an exclusive Catholic institution for girls in Purchase, New York. Inspired by John F. Kennedy, she volunteered in his presidential campaign as a teenager. Upon her graduation from Manhattanville in 1967, she obtained a position in Robert F. Kennedy's senatorial office. That led to her very responsible duties in the boiler room of RFK's ill-fated run for the Democratic nomination for president in 1968. Later she obtained a law degree, married, and practiced law in a partnership with her husband in Lincoln, Massachusetts. She was willing to be interviewed for Bill Kurtis's *Investigative Reports: Chappaquiddick* on A&E in recent years but was asked only softball questions.

The accident posed a huge problem for Kennedy's political career. He knew that a police officer had seen him (or, at least, a man) and a woman in his Olds 88 very shortly before the wreck, which likely would be regarded as the result of negligent or even reckless driving. And the car would be identified as his. He knew how damaging that could be if he had to explain the escapade on national television — particularly with his wife at home, pregnant. He *had* to avoid that.

Upon arriving back at the cottage, Kennedy, not wishing to be seen dripping wet, called from near the roadway to LaRosa, who was sitting on the ground just outside the cottage. Kennedy asked him to bring Gargan and Markham out to see him. Recognizing the voice but not the form standing beyond the Valiant, LaRosa complied only after the request was repeated.[10]

Later inquest testimony agrees that Kennedy was alone when he called to LaRosa. What happened to his companion, who the abandoned handbag suggests was Rosemary Keough? The absence of a surviving companion at this point has previously discouraged speculation about the existence of such a person. But new analysis of inquest testimony,

Joseph Gargan, cousin of Ted Kennedy   *Paul F. Markham, onetime U.S. attorney*
(Associated Press)   *for Massachusetts* (Associated Press)

presented in chapter 8, strikingly illuminates the existence of a companion, her absence at that moment, and her identity!

Gargan and Markham emerged from the cottage to find Kennedy slumped down in the backseat of the Valiant, parked beyond the rail fence near the roadway. *The strategy worked out in the next half-hour to free Kennedy from responsibility for what they then thought was just a one-car, unobserved, no-significant-injury automobile accident would turn out to entrap him in a far worse predicament.*

From Kennedy's privileged point of view, the solution to the problem was obvious: he was not going to take responsibility for it. Someone else should be willing to admit being the driver, and he, Kennedy, needed to establish an alibi as being back in Edgartown.

It is clear from their long friendship and family relationship that Kennedy would expect his cousin Gargan to take the fall for him for this simple bit of poor driving, as he then regarded the episode to be. After all, there was no lighting at the bridge, it abruptly angled to the left, it had no guardrails, and no one saw how fast the car was going. *Why would he not be willing to say he was the driver and lone occupant?* Kennedy must have thought. His thinking was rooted in the nature of his long, close, but unequal relationship with Gargan.[11]

Gargan's mother died when he was six, so he was reared in the working-class household of an aunt and uncle. An invitation to vacation at the Kennedys' elegant home at Hyannis Port, on the south shore of Cape Cod, as a playmate for eight-year-old Teddy began their long friendship. Not only was Joey two years older than Teddy, but his upbringing and nature made him capable of doing many ordinary chores that Teddy should, but could not, handle. An implicit three-way bargain began: the Kennedy parents were happy to have Joe around to look after Ted, Joe enjoyed the Kennedy lifestyle and was happy to handle Ted's shortcomings, and Ted was happy to have an always accommodating friend. Gargan's father's death when Gargan was sixteen strengthened his attachment to the Kennedy family. Rose, Ted's mother, saw to it that Gargan, her sister's son, obtained a prep-school and college education.[12] Ted's friendly dependence on Joe continued into adulthood. Gargan, who became a practicing attorney, an assistant U.S. attorney in the early 1960s, and a vice president of a Hyannis bank, nevertheless found time to work in Kennedy's senatorial campaigns. Gargan handled many subordinate duties, particularly those of a trusted personal advance man, arranging political appearances.

Kennedy's thinking as he sat in the Valiant late that night must have been, *Gargan is family and should be willing to protect the Kennedy senatorial seat and presidential ambitions.* One can imagine Kennedy saying, "Look, Joe, it's just a simple one-car accident. Nobody saw it. Nobody was hurt. You can say you just borrowed my car and drove off alone for a refreshing swim at East Beach. Okay? [He probably did not mention his encounter with Deputy Sheriff Look.] You don't have to mention the party. Just say you didn't see the bridge angling to the left and drove off it. You got out, were uninjured, and walked back to the cottage. There is no need to report the accident until tomorrow morning. Okay? You can go look at the scene in the morning so you can describe it accurately. Joe, I can't have the bad press. They'll start writing about my drinking again. I've got an election next year, and '72 is not that far off. I'll be in Edgartown when you say it happened. With you as the driver, the story won't go beyond the local paper." Such privileged, entitled thinking had undoubtedly been ingrained in Ted by his domineering father, who was often quoted as having said, "Look, I spent a lot of money for that Senate seat. It belongs in the family."

Gargan has related that Nance Lyons did, in fact, suggest that he claim to be the driver, but he firmly rejected the idea.[13] But that conversation occurred after Mary Jo's drowning was known to all, and the accident could no longer be thought of as a one-car, unobserved crash that resulted in no significant injuries. At least the record shows that such thoughts and discussions did occur. More to the point, Jack Anderson, in his syndicated column about three weeks after the accident, claimed that "most reliable sources" told him that following the accident, Kennedy decided "he would ask his cousin, Joe Gargan, to take the rap for him."[14] Also, when the Boston Globe Spotlight Team reinvestigated the accident in 1974, they wrote, "In particular, Kennedy's cousin, Joseph Gargan, agreed at one point to take responsibility for the accident, the source said."[15] Gargan also described later how Kennedy continued to resist reporting the accident to the police after Mary Jo's death was made known to him and after realizing that no one would then take the fall for him. And Gargan has been frank in saying, "We were . . . trying to get the story together prior to reporting the accident."[16] "Get the story together" implies creative fabrication more than memory organization.

But the key observation — again, one by disinterested observers — is Kennedy's relaxed, natural, untroubled behavior the next morning in Edgartown, which clearly demonstrated that he felt he was "home free." Someone else, not he, would take responsibility for the simple, unobserved, one-car, no-injury automobile accident — *the only problem then known to him.*

To complete the scheme, Kennedy had Gargan and Markham drive him in the Valiant to the ferry slip. The *On Time* was docked across the channel, having made its last run earlier. The ferry actually had run later than usual that night but had shut down at 12:40 A.M., though the ferryman puttered around the craft on the Edgartown side until 1:20 A.M. Kennedy made no mention in his police statement the next morning of how he crossed the channel, but since it had to be a surreptitious return to Edgartown to establish his alibi, he could not simply use the public, ferry-shed pay phone to call the ferryman, whose phone number was posted there specifically for out-of-hours transits.

In his televised address a week later, Kennedy claimed for the first time, "I suddenly jumped into the water and impulsively swam across." Gargan much later described it more graphically in inquest testimony: "The Senator got out of the back seat of the car, took three steps and dove into the water and started to swim across the cut."[17] Thus, he was apparently fully clothed and shod. With clothing, shoes, and the back brace he had to wear from a 1964 plane crash acting as a strong drag on swimming, and with strong tidal inflow at that hour through the channel (high tide there did not occur until close to 4:00 A.M.), that would require very strong swimming for a person with chronic back trouble who had just struggled out of a submerged wreck. Gargan, however, later testified, "The Senator can swim that five or six times both ways. . . . The real form of exercise for the Senator since the back injury is swimming."[18] Nevertheless, suspicions about Kennedy's swimming claim in his TV speech were widely expressed. Jack Anderson reported in his column that "Gargan and Markham rustled up a boat and delivered Kennedy to the other side,"[19] a plausible but less heroic way of getting across — if the word *heroic* can apply to preparing a false alibi. *Whatever the method, Kennedy's fleeing to Edgartown to have an alibi proves he was planning on someone else taking the responsibility for the accident.*

A report stimulated by Anderson's column may give substance to the account of another boat. A participant in the Edgartown Yacht

Club Regatta, C. Remington Ballou, was on his yawl *Sumatra*, moored just inside the harbor, close to, but south of, the *On Time*'s crossing route on that Friday night. A short while before 2:00 A.M., he heard a hushed conversation coming from a nearby passing dinghy carrying three persons. The dinghy acted suspiciously by turning off its motor and lights and drifting. After apparently interacting with a larger boat that motored at that time out of the harbor to the Chappaquiddick beach near the ferry slip, the dingy turned its motor and lights back on and headed northward (the shortest crossing is westward to busy Edgartown center). Ballou's observations end there.[20]

A northward (and a bit eastward) heading is directly at the Edgartown Light beach, which juts out into the harbor and offered an inconspicuous landing spot for Kennedy. He erroneously claimed in later inquest testimony that the tide swept him out toward that beach. But the tide was strongly inflowing at 1:30 A.M.! This undermines the credibility of the whole swimming-the-channel story. He did testify that he landed at the "beach," which could only mean the Edgartown Light beach, because south of that the Edgartown shore is a forest of piers and retaining walls. The crossing to the Edgartown Light beach is well over twice as far as a direct crossing, but it was an optimum route for a surreptitious boat crossing.

Circumstantial evidence that came out at the inquest might support the Ballou report. Gargan testified that upon arrival in Edgartown with Kennedy's sailboat, *Victura*, on Thursday afternoon, July 17, "the harbor was at that time rather crowded and I anchored the boat almost directly across from the Edgartown Yacht Club but out of the channel and on the other side."[21] That puts Kennedy's boat rather close to the Ballou boat and the Chappaquiddick ferry slip. Also, Markham testified he saw the *Victura* crew leaving the boat in a dinghy after the Friday-afternoon race.[22]

Thus a possible explanation of Kennedy's crossing of the harbor could be that he swam the short distance (with the tide) to *Victura*, took the dinghy moored with it, returned to pick up Gargan and Markham, and asked young crewmember Howie Hall to move the *Victura* beyond the *On Time* ferry channel and close to Chappaquiddick for later rendezvous. The three then quietly motored across to the shore, choosing the beach at the Edgartown Light as it was dark and isolated, and discharged Kennedy. Gargan and Markham went back to the *Victura* and were taken ashore on Chappaquiddick by Hall, who then returned to the *Victura*.

This assumes that Hall slept on the boat that night. At the time, the Edgartown Yacht Club had a rule that regatta crews were to sleep on their boats.[23] While it is not surprising that Kennedy felt he could violate the rule, he could well have expected Hall to abide by it. Apparently Hall was never interviewed about this plausible crossing scenario at the time.

A recent interview with Howie Hall by the author, however, has yielded only a denial of this scenario.[24] Hall said he spent the Friday night at an unspecified Edgartown hotel, not on the *Victura*, after a night of partying with other young men. Further, he said that the *Victura* had no dinghy with it, contradicting Markham's observation, and that he used the harbormaster's launch to reach the shore.

Kennedy, successfully across the channel to Edgartown by whatever means, walked the four blocks or so from Edgartown Light beach down North Water Street to the Shiretown Inn. Unnoticed at the late hour, he entered his room and changed into fresh clothes. Then, to establish his alibi, he came out of his room onto its deck and down the exterior rear stairway, where he encountered Russell Peachey, the Shiretown Inn manager, patrolling the property to avert any regatta-weekend shenanigans.[25] Peachey was standing next to the office on the walkway beside the inn as Kennedy turned from the stairway toward him. Recognizing Kennedy, he asked if he could help in any way. Kennedy, exhibiting no signs of injury, shock, or concussion, said no, showing once again he had no intention of reporting the accident. Kennedy then complained about being awakened by noise supposedly coming from a party in an adjoining unit, but he was dressed in slacks and jacket, not pajamas, and he made no request to have the noise abated. Then saying he had misplaced his watch, he asked Peachey the time. Peachey, looking at the clock through the window of the office, gave it as 2:25 A.M. Knowing that the accident would be reported as having occurred well after midnight when the ferry was no longer running, Kennedy was then confident that his alibi was established and his "problem" was well taken care of.

Kennedy had a short and restless night, as his harrowing experience could well cause, but he was up, nattily dressed, and in the Shiretown Inn's office shortly after 7:00 A.M. to reserve a couple of newspapers and make a phone call from the inn's public telephone. The front-desk clerk, Frances Stewart, found him "normal in every way."[26] His call was to a woman with whom he was romantically involved and who would know the number of Kennedy's then-traveling brother-in-law, Steven Smith, the real leader at the time of the Kennedy clan.[27] (Ted's father, Joseph, the longtime leader, had had a disabling stroke in 1961 and died later in 1969.) After the call, Kennedy returned to the walkway between the Shiretown and Colonial inns toward his room. There he encountered his sailing friends Ross Richards and Stan Moore. Together they climbed the stairway to the deck that served both Kennedy's and Richards's rooms. They talked for ten or fifteen minutes, mostly about the previous day's race, which Richards had won. Then Ross's wife emerged from their room in anticipation of breakfast. They all chatted for another quarter-hour, with Kennedy as relaxed and affable as usual. Nothing in his speech, manner, or appearance seemed out of the ordinary, according Ross. Kennedy obviously was confident that what he thought was his simple automobile accident was all taken care of. At the sound of the inn's eight-o'clock breakfast bell, the Richardses asked whether Kennedy would join them for breakfast. He declined but said he might join them later.

Back at the Cottage

The night back at the Chappaquiddick cottage had not been pleasant. Party hilarity lasting long after midnight had trumped the participants' intention of returning to their comfortable Edgartown and Katama accommodations for the night. Only Kennedy was back in Edgartown. The others, except for Crimmins and Markham, had brought no overnight bags. Crimmins, who had tried to clear the

partygoers out before midnight, had gone to bed soon after. By 2:00
A.M., the other partygoers began filling the remaining three beds, the
couch, and the floor for an uncomfortable and short night's sleep.
Just what they supposed had happened to Mary Jo is left unknown.
Gargan, returning along with Markham around 2:00 A.M., answered
the others' limited curiosity by saying she was back at Katama Shores.
All things considered, it appears Gargan knew nothing about her actual
whereabouts at that time and probably learned of her absence only then
at the cottage. In his guarded remarks, he somehow left the impression
that she had crossed on the ferry in Kennedy's car, in spite of also saying
that Kennedy had swum the channel and was back at the Shiretown Inn.
In their late-night foggy thinking, several of the young women accepted
this nonsensical explanation. Gargan did not mention that an auto
accident had occurred that night. With nothing to do at the late hour to
clarify the confusion, it was time for everyone to catch a few winks.

Gargan and Markham probably had the least restful sleep as they
awaited morning. They had had no role in the accident but had been
pulled — uncomfortably — into its aftermath. Markham, in fact,
testified at the later inquest that what sleep he got was dozing in the
front seat of the Valiant and that he arose between 4:00 and 4:30 A.M.[28]
That is a nervous night. As dawn broke, the two of them must have
headed for Dike Bridge. It was important to be familiar with the crash
scene if it fell on Gargan to take responsibility for the accident, as all the
evidence points to. Arriving there, they found that, because of the air
bubble that had remained trapped in the trunk, the rear end of the car
was elevated and near the surface, and the incoming tidal current had
twisted the car almost 180 degrees so that it now faced the bridge.

Gargan and Markham must have been puzzled about the previous
night's happenings ever since their late-night return to the cottage.
They had helped Kennedy set up his alibi to escape responsibility for
his supposedly simple auto accident. Kennedy had probably told them
that he had had a companion who had also survived the crash, but it is
possible they had not been told her identity (see chapter 8). But back
at the cottage they had learned of another unusual occurrence that
evening: Mary Jo was missing! They knew nothing about that. And,

likely, they had not even gotten all their thinking together on their role in Kennedy's alibi, so they had not mentioned the accident. Saying Mary Jo was all right, back at her motel, was the only way to avoid more questions, even if it was nonsense in relation to their tale of Kennedy swimming the channel. No wonder the young women later gave such confusing testimony on those late-night remarks.

Common sense would suggest that two odd happenings in a small group in a short time might be related. If Kennedy had not revealed his front-seat companion to Gargan and Markham, they could have easily wondered whether it were the missing Mary Jo. They could well have approached the Dike Bridge the next morning with eerie premonitions. Could Mary Jo have been in the car? Was she still there? What else could have happened to her?

Such puzzlement must have led them to enter the water to inspect the wreck. Gargan and Markham must have stripped down, jumped in, and — shockingly — caught a glimpse of Mary Jo's body — perhaps a foot in the rear window or a leg in a rear side window! Kennedy had said *nothing* to them about Mary Jo being with him in the car. Gargan, especially, must have been shocked, upset, and angry. *What sort of a rap is Kennedy trying to pass off on me?* Gargan must have thought. With nothing to dry himself off, he hurriedly climbed back into his clothing and did not even think about his disheveled hair.

With daybreak near 5:30 A.M., no one in the nearby houses was awake to notice Gargan and Markham's exploration of the wreckage. They climbed into the Valiant and returned to the cottage to anxiously await the first return trip of the *On Time,* which began service at 7:00 A.M. that day, a half-hour earlier than usual. Because he had not intended to stay at the cottage overnight, Gargan had no change of clothes available. Neither Gargan nor Markham revealed Mary Jo's death to anyone at the cottage. When Gargan and Markham were about to leave for the ferry, Tretter, Rosemary Keough, and Susan Tannenbaum asked to go along, and they agreed, but there was no conversation as the group tensely headed to the ferry slip. They left the Valiant on the Chappaquiddick side and took the *On Time* over to Edgartown as pedestrians. Off the ferry, they hurried the two blocks to the Shiretown Inn. Separating from the others, who went to Tretter's room, Gargan and Markham went to the rear of the inn and up the stairs to the deck of Mayberry House. There was Kennedy, amiably chatting with the Richardses as if nothing had happened.

In reconstructing events, particularly at this moment, we put much emphasis on Kennedy's demeanor at each stage of his ordeal, as a key to understanding what occurred. For this, we find support in Max Lerner's insightful biography of Kennedy, *Ted Kennedy and the Kennedy Legend*, when he wrote, "Those who have studied Chappaquiddick have been so absorbed with the inconsistencies and gaps in Ted's story that they have lost sight of what counts. With so many gaps in what he said he did, it is better to start with his state of mind and emotions and use it to reconstruct his actions."[29]

Marilyn Richards later described Gargan at that moment: "Joey looked awful. His clothes were all wrinkled, his hair was sticking out."[30] Both Marilyn and Ross Richards also described Gargan and Markham as "soaking wet" in an interview with Lt. John Dunn of the district attorney's office.[31] In his inquest testimony, Ross modified his account, saying, "They were ruffled looking. I would say they looked damp. Their hair hadn't been combed in some time."[32] But Marilyn, who was not called at the inquest, held to their earlier description.[33] When Ross toned down his description of Gargan and Markham at the inquest, Judge Boyle curiously intervened in the questioning to prevent Ross's earlier account from being introduced as evidence. Gargan has described himself similarly at that moment, but with a twist, stating, "I was soaking wet, because it was a hot, muggy morning [at 8:00 A.M.?] and I was very agitated and eager to find out what the hell was going on."[34]

The last clause clearly indicates that Gargan had known nothing about Mary Jo's drowning until that morning and was anxiously trying to make sense of what he knew and learn what had actually happened. He must have been very angry, thinking that Kennedy had tried to entrap him with the responsibility for a death, rather than just a one-car, unobserved automobile accident with no injuries. Brusquely interrupting the pleasantries on the deck, Gargan demanded to speak to Kennedy in private. Finding that Kennedy had locked himself out of his room, Gargan retrieved another key from the office, and the three of them, Markham included, went in.

In his room, Kennedy was stunned to learn of Mary Jo's fate. He had had no inkling whatsoever that she was in the backseat of his car as he and his front-seat companion had roared down Dike Road for East Beach. Mary Jo apparently had realized she had had too much to drink at the party, left the cottage unobtrusively, climbed into the backseat of the commodious Kennedy car, lay down, and dozed off or passed out. She was known among her friends as a light drinker, but for whatever reason — the gaiety of a special party on a special regatta weekend with a senator's entourage, or perhaps the need to release some tension in her private life — she imbibed more than usual that night, more than was wise, more than she could handle. She had to slip out from the party.

There were hints of stressful events in her private life that could account for her out-of-character drinking. She had confided to her mother, Gwen, sometime previously that she hoped to marry her boyfriend, who worked for the Foreign Service in Washington.[35] But ominously, in a phone call to her mother the evening before leaving for the regatta weekend, she said she had reached two important decisions.[36] At just that moment, the conversation was interrupted when her father, Joseph, arrived home and joined the phone call. Somehow in the following, meandering, three-way conversation, what those two decisions were never came up. And they never will be known. But they hint at tensions that could have caused Mary Jo to unconsciously seek alcohol — that great relaxer — to relieve.

The blood-alcohol level later found in Mary Jo's body (0.09 percent) indicated an intake of three to four drinks in the hour or so before her death. That's enough for a five-foot-two, 110-pound female to be pretty inebriated, contrary to the protective testimony of her friends at the later inquest. Perhaps when Kennedy stopped his car on Cemetery Road, then abruptly backed up as Deputy Look approached, Mary Jo was aroused enough to rise up momentarily before lying back down, which could account for Look's uncertain observation of someone in the backseat.

Who was Mary Jo Kopechne, whose name was to become as well known as Liz Taylor's at the time? She was a pretty, blond, petite, trim young woman, about to turn twenty-nine, who had gone to Washington to contribute to the liberal agenda of the 1960s. Though described by her friends in her early years in Washington as unsophisticated, gentle, naïve, quiet, or nice, Mary Jo had matured in her six years there into a socially and professionally confident young woman.[37] Her love of dancing had even led some friends to call her "Salome," but she remained very proper, some might say even prim. Her first job there was in the office of George Smathers, the three-term Democratic senator from Florida. With his recommendation, Mary Jo obtained a position in newly elected senator Robert F. Kennedy's office in 1965. She admired Bobby Kennedy greatly and soon became a trusted aide. When he ran for the Democratic nomination for president in 1968, she was entrusted with a position in the heart of his campaign effort, the boiler room, where she oversaw delegate support in Delaware, Kentucky, and Pennsylvania. Devastated by his assassination in June of that year, she found comfort in the friendship of the other five young women working in the boiler room.

Mary Jo was born in Pennsylvania but grew up in Berkeley Heights, New Jersey. She graduated with a degree in business administration from Caldwell College for Women in Caldwell, New Jersey, a small, Catholic, liberal-arts college. She was very popular, participated in campus activities such as the debate club and yearbook, worked in the library for all four years, and showed an interest in politics and international affairs.[38] After she graduated in 1962, her deep Roman Catholic beliefs led her to volunteer for a year at the Mission of St. Jude in Montgomery, Alabama, teaching impoverished African-American children as her contribution to the Civil Rights Movement.

Gossip columnists, making too much of a party of six young, single women and six older, married (except Crimmins) men, left an impression of Mary Jo as a "party girl." In reaction to that, other writers wanted to grant her sainthood for her strong religious beliefs and idealistic political commitment. (She had, in fact, seriously considered becoming a nun at one time.) But her close boiler-room friend,

Mary Jo Kopechne, who died in the Kennedy automobile accident (©
Bettmann/CORBIS)

Rosemary Keough, offered a more balanced portrait. Mary Jo was a "normal, red-blooded American girl" who was energetic, witty, and politically commited.[39]

From the confrontation in Kennedy's room, muffled but heated words were heard outside. Gargan may well have angrily accused Kennedy of trying to push responsibility for Mary Jo's death on him, but Kennedy's startled reaction must have made it apparent that he was as surprised and shocked by the discovery as Gargan and Markham had been. The frenzied discussion continued for twenty minutes or more because Tretter, who had been to his room at the Shiretown to shower and shave, then came up on the deck and knocked on Kennedy's door. Thinking that Kennedy had indicated through the window for him to come in, Tretter opened the door and stepped in, only to be told rather brusquely by Kennedy that the conversation was private and he should leave. In his inquest testimony, Tretter later described Kennedy at that moment as "angry or disturbed"[40] and said that "in his eyes and in his face there was something wrong"[41] — a clear demonstration of Kennedy's abrupt change of demeanor and mood upon learning of Mary Jo's drowning. When Kennedy emerged from the room a few minutes later, he was a changed man, no longer amiable and relaxed but upset, grim, anxious, and troubled.

Kennedy, in psychological, but not physical, shock at the news, grasped for a way out. The crash was no longer the simple auto accident that he had arranged to avoid responsibility for. It was a fatal accident, and he would have to own up to being the driver! Not even a close cousin would take the rap for anything as serious as that. Kennedy's first thought was to claim that Mary Jo was driving.[42] The trouble was he knew that an officer (Deputy Look) had seen him (or at least a man) driving his car just minutes before the crash. And he did not even know at the moment whether Mary Jo had a driver's license.

A new story was needed.

Chapter 3
The New Story

The original false scenario and alibi that Kennedy had set up to avoid all involvement in the accident now entrapped him. He still wished to avoid the appearance of an amorous adventure, but now he had to explain why he had not sought help to save Mary Jo, why he had not reported the fatal accident immediately, and why he had fled to Edgartown. And no one was going to take the rap for him. He had initially schemed to cover up his attempted tryst, but now he had to cover up that and the dishonesty of the attempted alibi, a worse sin for a politician.

Slowly, at the repeated urging of Gargan and Markham, Kennedy realized he would have to take responsibility for the accident and report it. But he held back, unwilling to accept the "new" reality and hoping to find a way out. It was a hell of an adjustment! His mind was in "a jumble of emotions — grief, fear, doubt, exhaustion, panic, confusion, and shock," as Kennedy described himself in his later television address.[1] What could he say happened? What was a believable scenario that he could offer? He needed ideas and advice. The truth, certainly, was now out of the question. He needed to call several associates, but where could he do that in private? His thoughts and conversation, he knew, must not be heard outside his tight circle of advisers. Gargan suggested the payphone in the ferry shed, a modest little waiting room with bare wooden benches on the Chappaquiddick side, so Kennedy, Gargan, and Markham went off on foot to the ferry.

It was already about 8:30 A.M. The Richardses, returning from breakfast, observed Kennedy's changed demeanor as the three men passed them. "They were obviously in a big rush, and looked very preoccupied. They passed us without a greeting," Marilyn Richards has stated.[2] From the ferry shed, Kennedy first called David Burke, who after three years as his administrative assistant in Washington was a trusted confidant. He also phoned K. Dun Gifford, a legislative assistant in his Senate office, and tried unsuccessfully to reach the Kennedy family attorney, Burke Marshall. Gifford, then at the family home on nearby Nantucket Island, immediately called a local pilot and within fifteen minutes was airborne.[3] Before nine o'clock, the plane swooped over Dike Bridge, and Gifford saw Kennedy's car still in the water. He muttered to himself, "My God! There goes Ted's presidency right there."[4] The comment, while prophetic, also reveals that Gifford already knew the full extent of the tragedy.

While Kennedy was on the phone, Gargan took the Valiant, parked on the Chappaquiddick side, and headed for the cottage. Along the way, he found the Lyons sisters, Esther Newburgh, Ray LaRosa, and Jack Crimmins walking toward the ferry. He picked them up and drove on to the cottage. At the later inquest, Nance Lyons described the situation as they climbed into the car:[5]

> Assistant District Attorney Armand Fernandes, Jr.: What was the conversation at this time, as best you can remember it, between the parties?
>
> A. Lyons: Well, I can only relate my reaction at the time and I knew that looking at Mr. Gargan's face I knew that something was wrong and I said, "Is something wrong," and he said, "Yes, get in the car." And we got in the car and we all began asking, "What happened, what is wrong," and he said, "There's been an accident," and someone asked if the Senator had been hurt and he said, "No," and at that point I knew that something had happened to Mary Jo.
>
> Fernandes: What did you say?
>
> A. Lyons: I asked if anything happened to Mary Jo.
>
> Fernandes: What did he say?
>
> Lyons: He didn't answer. He just said we will return to the cottage.

There Gargan broke the news — partially — that there had been an automobile accident at Dike Bridge and that Mary Jo was missing. He insisted he had no more details. Then, thinking in a damage-control mode, he left Crimmins and LaRosa to clean the cottage of all evidence of a drinking party, while he took the three young women to the ferry with instructions to take a taxi to their motel. Arriving at Katama Shores, the Lyons sisters and Newburgh hoped to find Mary Jo there. When they did not, there was consternation, but there was nothing to do but to sit, wait, and worry.

Later, Gargan returned to the cottage to take the two men and all the party debris away from Chappaquiddick. Still later in the morning, he went back to the Katama Shores motel to tell the boiler-room gals — all five were then there — that Mary Jo had drowned, that Kennedy had been the driver, and that the accident had been reported to the police. Understandably, they took the news very emotionally. Gargan still remained mum on details. Much later, he explained he did not "want to say anything to these girls that would compromise whatever statement he [Kennedy] was making [to the police]."[6] "Whatever statement" is a clear admission by Gargan, years later, that he had no idea what story Kennedy was concocting for the police and that Gargan placed no trust in its credibility.

Near the end of the hour that Kennedy spent on the phone at the ferry shed, a wrecker with red lights flashing crossed on the ferry, a sure indication that the submerged wreck had been discovered. Also, the ferry operator, Richard Hewitt, having heard that the sunken automobile belonged to Kennedy and thinking that he and his friends there must not know of the accident, informed them of it. As Kennedy simply turned and walked away, Markham replied, "Yes, we just heard about it."[7] Clearly, reporting the accident could be postponed no longer.

Gargan, Markham, and Kennedy took the next crossing of the *On Time* back to Edgartown. Markham then accompanied Kennedy into police headquarters. The policewoman on duty in the office, Carmen Salvador, later said Kennedy appeared "very shaken, and he looked concerned and confused . . . and he looked as if he was really nervous,"[8] a further confirmation of Kennedy's drastically altered demeanor from his affable self early that morning.

The two had just arrived at the station when Police Chief Dominick James "Jim" Arena called from Dyke House, asking for someone to locate Kennedy. Kennedy was put on the telephone and heard Arena say,[9] "I am sorry. I have some bad news. Your car was in an accident over here and the young lady is dead."

"I know," replied Kennedy.

Arena, stunned at the unexpected and matter-of-fact reply, asked, "Can you tell me, was there anybody else in the car?"

"Yes," Kennedy answered.

Arena asked, "Are they in the water?"

"No," replied Kennedy, *tacitly and inadvertently acknowledging that more than himself had been in the car with the dead woman.*

Arena asked, "Can I talk to you?"

Kennedy responded, "Yes," and then said he preferred to talk at the police station. They agreed to meet as soon as Arena could get there. The police cruiser was needed at the accident scene, but a surgeon vacationing on Chappaquiddick, Dr. Edward Self, had just arrived at the bridge in his jeep to see what the commotion was about and, when asked, was glad to give Arena a lift to the ferry.

Arena, a former Marine sergeant and state trooper, was a strongly built, six-foot-four man with an imposing appearance in his uniform. He arrived at his office, however, in a wet bathing suit, dripping T-shirt, and bare feet at around 10:30 A.M. to find Kennedy and Markham waiting. Having had his questioning cut off on the phone and with a few minutes to gather his thoughts, Arena would be

Dominick James "Jim" Arena, chief of Edgartown Police (© JP Laffont/ Sigma/CORBIS)

expected to renew his questioning. Unfortunately, his accommodating personality led him to be so deferential in the presence of a United States senator and a member of the Kennedy clan that Kennedy determined their interaction throughout that crucial first day.

Gargan avoided being at the police station during the filing of Kennedy's report because he worried about its truthfulness and wished to be disassociated from it. In fact, when Leo Damore asked him in an interview why he had revealed so little about the accident that morning to the boiler-room girls, Gargan said, "I had very little knowledge about the accident itself, except for Paul and I doing the diving. How much of any of that the Senator is going to tell the police I do not know."[10] Gargan here again freely admitted he had no idea what story Kennedy would fabricate.

In his office, Arena was stunned to hear Kennedy readily admit he was the driver in the fatal accident and that the dead young woman was not Rosemary Keough, as Arena had supposed from finding her handbag in the automobile, but instead was "Miss Mary" (whose full name Kennedy could not provide). Despite finding a third person's handbag in the car and having heard Kennedy seem to agree, only minutes before, that there were more than two people in the car, Arena failed to explore that totally obvious avenue of inquiry. Arena's reticence at that moment would characterize his entire investigation. Would not a natural question at that point have been, "Was Keough in the car at the time of the crash? And if not, who was the other person or persons?" Or, "How did the handbag get in the car?" Almost any answer would have led Arena to learn of the party and its guests and then to question them that day, before they were hurried off the island. Arena's lack of connecting Keough to Kennedy became all the more stunning when Arena testified at the later inquest that he had found "a United States Senate card identifying Rosemarie Keough as an employee of the United States Senate"[11] in her handbag inside the wreck. (Others have identified it as an admission pass to the Senate.) Not exploring right then Keough's possible involvement in the accident was the investigation's most serious omission. Within the hour, in his written statement, Kennedy would deny the presence of a third party in the car.

Surprisingly, Arena did not initiate *any* questioning of Kennedy about the accident. Instead, he agreed to allow Kennedy to make a written statement, going as far as finding Kennedy an empty office for privacy. There Kennedy dictated a statement to Markham, apparently with the latter's legal advice on every sentence, since it took about an hour to compose the 247-word handwritten statement.

During that time Arena returned to the accident scene. Arriving back at police headquarters, he found Kennedy's statement nearly completed (except for filling in Kopechne's full name). With the policewoman typist busy answering the phone, Arena himself typed the statement in duplicate. It read:

> On July 18, 1969 at approximately 11:15 P.M. in Chappaquiddick, Martha's Vineyard, Massachusetts, I was driving my car on Main Street on my way to get the ferry back to Edgartown. I was unfamiliar with the road and turned right onto Dike Road, instead of bearing hard left on Main Street. After proceeding approximately one-half mile on Dike Road I descended a hill and came upon a narrow bridge. The car went off the side of the bridge. There was one passenger with me, one Miss Mary [Jo Kopechne, added later], a former secretary of my brother Sen. Robert Kennedy. The car turned over and sank into the water and landed with the roof resting on the bottom.
>
> I attempted to open the door and the window of the car but have no recollection of how I got out of the car. I came to the surface and then repeatedly dove down to the car in an attempt to see if the passenger was still in the car. I was unsuccessful in the attempt. I was exhausted and in a state of shock.
>
> I recall walking back to where my friends were eating. There was a car parked in front of the cottage and I climbed into the backseat. I then asked someone to bring me back to Edgartown. I remember walking around for a period and going back to my hotel room. When I fully realized what had happened this morning, I immediately contacted the police.

While having Kennedy check over the typing of the statement (which Kennedy did not sign), Arena noted that he "appeared to be very depressed mentally,"[12] another observation of the drastic change in Kennedy's mood after the arrival of Gargan and Markham that morning. At this point, Arena, still in awe of the senator, made other errors of omission: He did not ask why Kennedy had not sought help immediately to rescue Mary Jo, who might have been alive and breathing in an air pocket; or why he had left the scene of a fatal accident; or why he had waited almost ten hours to report the accident; or what he had been doing during that time; or why he had fled to Edgartown. Instead, Arena readily agreed to withhold both questioning and release of the written statement until Kennedy had consulted with Burke Marshall, in the trusting — and mistaken — expectation that Kennedy would cooperate fully, presumably later that day. Of course, Kennedy could have refused to answer questions under that circumstance, but being a public person, he might have felt compelled at that time to explain at least some of his obviously peculiar behavior.

Kennedy's statement, "I recall walking back to where my friends were eating," should have alerted Arena to a party, prompting him to ask Kennedy about it. Unfortunately, Arena took another two days to realize that Kennedy had been at a party attended by eleven other people. Kennedy's choice of the word "eating," an activity that was long over at that hour, rather than the more accurate "partying" or the more uncomfortably frank "drinking," was enough to hide the gathering from Arena until reporters later brought it to his attention.

Kennedy's statement was received with wide disbelief. Could he have instead just told the truth? No; admitting to setting up a false alibi would have been worse for a politician than admitting to womanizing, but worse yet, the truth would be admitting to both. Lies uncovered must be recovered with new lies.

How did Kennedy arrive at this new story? First, he was forced to admit to being the driver. No one else would take the rap for him because it was now a fatal accident, and it was obvious that claiming Mary Jo was the driver would not work. Second, he had to come up with a proper reason to be driving with Mary Jo late at night in order to escape the charge of womanizing. The only choice was to claim they both had decided to leave the party and go to their separate rooms for the night and so were driving to the ferry before it shut down around midnight.

The falseness of that claim was revealed when Mary Jo's purse was found at the cottage. What young woman would head for her motel room without her purse and room key? And why would Mary Jo, having decided to leave the party, not inform any of her five companions staying at the Katama Shores Inn, particularly her roommate, Newburgh? That behavior is so completely unlikely that it is simply unbelievable. Further, if returning to their overnight accommodations were the purpose of their leaving the party, Kennedy would have had his regular chauffeur, Crimmins, drive them to the ferry, so that Crimmins could return the car for use by the ten partygoers still at the cottage. And why wouldn't they offer a ride to others at the party wishing to turn in? Kennedy clearly had in mind another purpose for the drive. Also, can anyone imagine Kennedy being so ill mannered and unsociable as to walk out on his own party without saying a word of explanation or even a "goodnight" to his guests?

To cover the lie of heading for the ferry meant lying about the time they left the party, so that it would be before the ferry's usual last trip of the night. Hence Kennedy claimed they left at 11:15 P.M. Maintaining this time required him to deny ever encountering Deputy Look at the Dike Road intersection at about 12:45 A.M., an account from a reliable witness too specific to be disbelieved (and later corroborated by both LaRosa's and the Lyons sisters' testimonies as well as the tidal flow direction).

Support for the later time has also come from Sylvia Malm, the then nineteen-year-old daughter named after her mother, who was awake and reading in her second-floor bedroom of Dyke House until midnight.[13] Her wide-open window faced directly toward the Dike Bridge. She maintained that, in the stillness of the night there, she could not have missed hearing a car drive by and plunge into Poucha Pond, had it occurred before midnight. Mrs. Malm, in a less strategically located bedroom but awake later than her daughter, said she heard a car go past between midnight and one o'clock.[14] Neither of the Malms were called at the inquest to offer this eyewitness information.

The new story also required Kennedy to explain why he turned onto the dirt and gravel Dike Road eastward, rather than following the paved, striped, and banked sharp turn of Chappaquiddick Road westward toward the ferry landing. Kennedy's calling Chappaquiddick Road "Main Street" in his statement unintentionally indicates an understanding of the layout of the few roads on Chappaquiddick. His understanding is further confirmed by his knowing the then *unposted* name of Dike Road, which he turned onto, and its distance of a half-mile from the Dike Bridge. And as already mentioned, he had been driven on Dike Road and across Dike Bridge the previous afternoon, as well as back to the ferry slip. To not notice the change in road surface immediately is simply not believable. Also, if Kennedy were really trying to catch the last ferry, his front-seat companion would likely have pointed out his "wrong turn." That night, he explained to Markham that he had made a wrong turn, but "he couldn't turn around,"[15] also unbelievable. Any driver can turn around on a two-lane road or, for convenience, use one of the several driveways present. These several considerations undermine the credibility of Kennedy's claim that he made a wrong turn because he was "unfamiliar with the road." Also, the remark seems to indicate that he was not fully open with Markham about his activities that night.

Kennedy's curious description of descending a "hill" to Dike Bridge can only be interpreted as impaired perception or memory or both, made fuzzy by too many rum and cokes. The road descends at a 1 percent slope (one foot down every hundred feet of travel) several hundred feet from the bridge, hardly a hill even from an ant's viewpoint.

Kennedy's claim that he made many attempts to rescue Mary Jo is entirely fictitious and an attempt to portray himself in a heroic role. His peculiar wording seems to convey, in fact, that he was still puzzled about Mary Jo's presence in the car at the time of writing. Would not normal wording simply have been, "repeatedly dove down to save Miss Mary" rather than "repeatedly dove down to the car in an attempt to see if the passenger was still in the car"? In reality, Kennedy did not dive to rescue a person he did not know was there.

Notice also the peculiar wording, "There was one passenger with me, one Miss Mary. . . . " A normal wording would have been, "Miss Mary was a passenger with me." Kennedy wished to make it doubly clear that there was just *one* passenger. Why was that so necessary to emphasize? His conversation with Arena on the phone just an hour earlier had implicitly and apparently inadvertently acknowledged that there was another person in the car besides himself and Mary Jo, so he now wished to deny that emphatically. Most likely, Kennedy had said he would keep his front-seat companion's name out of the accident report entirely in his originally planned alibi. He had had no opportunity to talk with that person since the revelation of Mary Jo's presence in the car, so he had no alternative but to keep her name out of the new story. Were he now to admit her presence, she might then decide to tell the truth and so reveal him not only as a lying womanizer but also as trying initially to arrange a false alibi. That dishonesty would certainly end his political career, so he could not now disclose her presence.

Kennedy's fabricated statement did not answer in any way other natural questions. Why had he not sought help in rescuing Mary Jo by going to Dyke House, where a backdoor light was lit, or to the cottage across the road, where a front bedroom light was lit, and calling for help? Why would he not have knocked — even hammered — on the door of either cottage, even if both were dark, as he later claimed in inquest testimony? Why did he not use the emergency alarm to summon help at the fire station that he passed on the walk back to the cottage? The only explanation is that he and his companion did not know that Mary Jo was in the car, gasping for her last breaths from a pocket of air. Kennedy was guilty of reckless driving and lying repeatedly about the wreck, but he was far from being so callous as to knowingly walk away from a trapped, dying person. He obviously did not know Mary Jo was in the car, and neither did his front-seat companion.

Why had the "someone" (of his police statement) back at the cottage not insisted on Kennedy reporting the accident right then, using the nearby fire station alarm? That scenario is plausible only if the incident was not known to be a fatal accident and was "being taken care of." Why had that "someone" been willing to help Kennedy get back to Edgartown? It apparently was part of an agreed-upon plan to disassociate Kennedy from the accident completely. Someone had agreed to be the lone driver in what was then thought to be a one-car, unobserved accident with no injuries. At least, Kennedy must have *believed* there was such an agreement. From their long, close friendship, he would have trusted that Gargan would consent to being identified as the driver, as discussed earlier.

Did Kennedy's description of himself as being "in a state of shock" and statement that he had not "fully realized what had happened" until the morning indicate he had suffered a concussion? No one, during the night of the wreck or the next day in Edgartown, observed or described his behavior as dazed, uncomprehending, or confused. These people include Gargan and Markham at the cottage soon after the accident; Peachey outside the Shiretown Inn at 2:25 A.M.; the front-desk clerk, Stewart, at the Shiretown Inn at 7:00 A.M.; Ross and Marilyn Richards on the deck at 7:30 A.M.; the *On Time* ferryman at 9:30 A.M.; and Chief Arena at 10:30 A.M. and then again at almost noon. A snapshot of Kennedy leaving the ferry slip in Edgartown at around 9:45 A.M., as he returned from phoning at the ferry shed, shows a vigorous person with a purposeful stride. Kennedy must certainly have been in a state of psychological shock but exhibited no signs of physiological shock or a concussion.

That did not stop his personal physician, Dr. Robert D. Watt of Hyannis, from giving Kennedy a helpful diagnosis of "concussion, contusions and abrasions of the scalp, [and] acute cervical strain"[16] later that day, upon Kennedy's return to his Hyannis Port home.

When was it that Kennedy "fully realized what had happened"? Clearly, it was when Gargan and Markham arrived at his room with the news of Mary Jo's fate, and his demeanor changed abruptly from amiable, casual, and relaxed to grim, tense, and troubled.

Had Kennedy then "immediately contacted the police"? No. Gargan and Markham arrived on Kennedy's deck about 7:45 A.M., and Kennedy did not begin to make a statement to Chief Arena until about 10:30 A.M. Kennedy had spent almost three hours seeking advice and counsel and fabricating his new story.

And it was far from a believable story. People sensed a cover-up, but they were puzzled about what was being covered up. Had something worse than a drowning occurred?

Chapter 4

The Accident Scene

Gargan and Markham had left Dike Bridge not long after daybreak, the evidence suggests, after diving in, exploring the sunken wreck, and shockingly discovering the body of Mary Jo Kopechne. Their activities had gone unnoticed at that early hour. They had rushed back to the cottage to await the first return trip of the *On Time* ferry into Edgartown, so that they could break the stunning news to Kennedy and seek an explanation.

On that first trip of the ferry coming to Chappaquiddick was a car containing a pair of fishermen, a young high-school science teacher, and a teenager vacationing from upstate New York, headed for East Beach to do some early-morning surf casting. Exiting the *On Time*, they took Chappaquiddick Road to Dike Road, passed over Dike Bridge, and parked short of the sand dune that forms East Beach. With their usual fickleness, the fish were not biting that morning, so after a fruitless hour of repeated casting off shore and reeling in their empty lines, they returned to their car at Dike Bridge and then decided to try their luck casting off the bridge.

They had hardly begun when a glint of the rising sun off the chrome of the barely submerged rear end of Kennedy's car caught the teacher's eye. Realizing what it was, they rushed to the nearest residence, Dyke House, where Mrs. Malm answered their anxious knock at the rear door. She immediately called an emergency number with the news. The operator relayed the information to the Edgartown police station, where Chief Arena received the call and decided instantly to handle the situation himself. It was then 8:20 A.M.

Arena jumped into his cruiser, found the *On Time* waiting at the slip, and arrived at the scene within minutes. First concerned about possible occupants of the car, he radioed for the fire department's water-rescue expert and also another Edgartown police officer to come posthaste. Having found before he left the station that there had been no accident report during the night, Arena was concerned that the driver and perhaps passengers might still be in the wreck. The rear tires of the overturned car were just beginning to break the surface, as the tide was going out. He felt compelled to get in the water immediately and look inside the car for occupants, hopefully survivors. Having no bathing suit, he jogged the hundred or so yards to Dyke House, where Mrs. Malm was happy to lend him her husband's swim trunks.

Hustling back to Dike Bridge, Arena jumped in the water and attempted to look into the automobile's rear and side windows. With little on the car to grasp near the rear windows, he found that the strong tidal flow overpowered his swimming abilities. And with no face mask, his several attempts at peering in the windows failed. He climbed onto the sunken car and sat on the edge of the rear bumper, which was just below the surface. From his perch he could make out the submerged Massachusetts license plate — L78 207 — and called it out to the newly arrived police officer, Robert Bruguiere, for him to radio in to learn the owner from the registration listing. Just a few minutes later, Arena was stunned when Bruguiere called out from the cruiser that the owner was Edward M. Kennedy!

The Edgartown fire chief, Antone Silva, and the department's water-rescue expert, John N. Farrar, had arrived along with Bruguiere. Farrar had received word of the accident at the Turf 'N Tackle shop in Edgartown, where he was manager, at 8:25 A.M. He immediately drove to the fire station a half-mile away to obtain his scuba equipment, climbed into the fire chief's car with Silva, and donned the gear on the way to the bridge. They arrived at Dike Bridge only twenty minutes after receiving the call, in spite of just missing a ferry departure, and Farrar immediately entered the water. Diving downward, he found the driver's-side door locked but its window wide open. With a clear view into the window opening through his goggles, he found no one in the front seat compartment. Fighting the tidal current, he maneuvered around the car. At the rear he was able to peer into the submerged, unbroken, rear window. There he saw two sandal-clad feet!

Farrar quickly moved to the passenger side of the overturned car, the side that had hit the water flat. Both of the side-door windows had been shattered inward by the impact. Reaching through the backseat window, he grasped the right thigh of the person in the car and immediately felt the hardness of rigor mortis. Any thought that he was in a rescue operation disappeared in that moment. With a death, he knew that his testimony would be an essential part of an investigation and hearing, so he observed carefully as he worked to extricate the body from the car through that blown-out window, avoiding shards of glass along the edge. It was the body of a petite, pretty, young woman, attractively and fully clothed in dark blue slacks, a long-sleeved white blouse, gold chain belt, and white sandals.[1]

Her body's frozen-in-death configuration seemed to cry out about her desperate final moments trying to breathe the air of life. Her head was cocked back so that her nose was at its highest possible point in the rear-seat foot well of the overturned car, in order to breathe that last pocket of air. Her knees were up against the rear seat cushion, with her legs extended toward the rear window. Her rigid fingers were still grasping the seat-cushion edge in a desperate attempt to hold her nose in the shrinking air pocket of the foot well. The backseat floor was below the doorsill in the car's normal orientation, and so it initially trapped a pocket of air in the overturned orientation. However, the tilt of the overturned car allowed it to seep out. In comments to the author, Farrar has said there was no air pocket left when he extracted the body.[2] Farrar emphasized that the body, evidencing buoyancy, had not sunk down in the car, as do drowning victims with their water-filled lungs.

As Farrar extricated the body through the blown-out window, he placed his safety line loosely around the body's neck, in case he had to let go because of the tidal current. As he moved the body through the water, he felt that it was "about one-quarter positively buoyant," he stated later in a newspaper interview. "There was still a little air left in her."[3] With Arena's aid, the body was lifted out of the water and onto

Arena's lap as he still sat on the overturned car. Though her mouth was open, her teeth were clenched in a final agony. No injuries of any kind were apparent to Farrar or Arena. A rowboat on a rope was pulled over to them and they placed the body in it. On shore, it was laid on a stretcher and carried to the cruiser. Farrar had spent only ten minutes in the water removing the body. From his first notification to body removal had been only thirty minutes.

Farrar again entered the water to inspect the overturned, sunken car more fully and to retrieve the gold chain belt that had slipped off the body during its extraction. Resting on the ceiling of the front seat was a fashionable, flowered handbag containing cosmetics, toiletries, and the driver's license of Rosemary Keough. Her room keys from the Katama Shores Motor Inn were also in it, and a call to the inn from the cruiser revealed that neither she nor any of a group of six young women had slept there the previous night. This led to an initial, tentative, and erroneous identification of the deceased woman as Keough. This information should have, but did not, trigger questions by Arena as to what, if any, connection the group of six — and especially Keough — had to the automobile accident. This omission prevented discovery during those crucial first few hours of relevant information that would soon be locked in uncooperating heads that fled the island.

Though Arena was slow to make a connection to the six young women, he knew from long experience how to handle a fatal automobile accident. He had the medical examiner, an undertaker, and a wrecker summoned and the Registry of Motor Vehicles notified of a fatal accident, as required by law.

The associate medical examiner of Edgartown, Dr. Donald R. Mills, on duty that day, arrived soon, along with an Edgartown undertaker named Eugene Frieh and his assistant, David Guay. The stretcher with the body was removed from the cruiser and placed to the side, away from the view of the small crowd that had formed. Mills proceeded to examine the body, checking for a possible skull fracture, lacerations, and abrasions but not finding any. There was some froth with traces of blood about the nose and mouth, apparently emanating from the nose. Apart from that, there was no evidence of any trauma. Pressure on the chest caused surprisingly small amounts of water to come out of the nose and mouth. He unbuttoned the blouse, examined the chest, and, as a matter of course, checked for a heartbeat, though the rigor mortis precluded any possibility of one. He pulled the slacks partway down to examine the abdomen and noted she was not wearing any panties. He put no importance on the latter, but it was enough, when known to the media, to trigger reports of an imagined sexual encounter in various scandal sheets. (The lack of an immediate autopsy, which could have negated such speculation, gave a longer life to such imaginings.) That short examination of the body, along with the circumstance of its recovery from a submerged vehicle, led Mills to conclude it was "an obvious and clear"[4] case of drowning or, as he was to write on the death certificate, "asphyxiation by immersion (overturned submerged automobile)." Guay, who did the embalming, later said the body had "no cuts, no bruises, no puncture wounds, no lacerations, no broken bones, no broken teeth, no broken fingernails."[5] Neither were there any tears in her clothing.

While Mills was examining the body, Jon Ahlbum was using a cable attached to his wrecker to right the Kennedy car in the water, as a first step in recovering it. As the car was rotated, Farrar noticed sizable bubbles of air surfacing, showing that there still had been air trapped somewhere in the overturned automobile. The outflowing tide, however, kept pushing the submerged car toward the bridge piling, so they decided to wait for low tide, which was to occur shortly at 11:30 A.M., to pull the car out. During this stage of extraction, the driver's-side rearview mirror was damaged as the car was pressed toward the piling.[6] This otherwise peculiar damage has inspired wild speculation in one book about an accident of the car earlier that night.

Arena had looked for skid marks on the sandy wooden planks of the bridge leading up to the gouges in the rub rail. Though he could see the paths of the tires, he could see no deposit of black tire rubber in the tracks, which he thought was necessary to define skid marks. Next, the Registry of Motor Vehicles inspector, George Kennedy (no relation), and his assistant, Robert Molla of the Oak Bluffs office, arrived to investigate the fatal accident, as required by law. Inspector Kennedy,

Rescue expert John N. Farrar inspecting the partly recovered Kennedy car (© Bettmann/CORBIS)

perhaps with a more highly trained eye, did identify the paths of the tires as showing skid marks of thirty-three and eighteen feet for the left and right rear tires respectively, beginning at the very start of the bridge. The tracks continued straight off the bridge, evidencing no attempt to turn leftward onto the bridge. Citing traffic before his arrival, Kennedy was unable to decide whether the tire tracks in the gravel approaching the bridge were skid marks or not. He measured the position of the car along and outward from the bridge. The obvious reorientation of the car (heading toward the bridge) and likely lateral motion caused by tidal flow during the night made those measurements of little value.

Deputy Look had received a call from the Communications Center about the accident and had his daughter and wife drop him off at Dike Bridge before they headed for "the point" in the family car to catch the *On Time* to Edgartown. When he offered his services to Chief Arena, Arena asked Look to help with traffic control. Look mentioned to

Arena, and a little later to Officer Bruguiere, that he had seen a car drive toward the bridge late the previous night with a man at the wheel, a front-seat woman passenger, and perhaps a third person in the backseat. When Arena learned he had to meet Kennedy at the police headquarters, he asked Look for a lift, only to find that Look's family had taken his car. Look spotted a friend, Dr. Self, with his jeep, and asked him to take Arena to the ferry. When Arena returned to the accident scene a half-hour later, again in Dr. Self's jeep, he told Look that the car belonged to Senator Kennedy. Look uttered, "Oh, my God."[7] Later, at low tide when the car was pulled rear first from Poucha Pond, Look recognized it as the one he had seen speed off toward the bridge the night before. He immediately reported that to Bruguiere.

The damage to Kennedy's Olds 88 was now fully apparent. After leaving the bridge, it had rotated in air to the right a full ninety degrees before the passenger side hit the water flush and with such force that both front and rear doors were crushed inward a few inches and their windows blown in, resulting in the small shards of tempered glass found inside the car. The top was broadly dented, indicating that the car had bounced off its right side, continued to rotate, and then struck the water flush on its roof before sinking in that inverted orientation. The front windshield was also extensively cracked — apparently, from the pattern of cracks, from the roof denting, not from contact with the occupants' heads — though the safety-glass lamination had held the windshield together. The driver's-side window was rolled down to within an inch of the sill, indicating Kennedy's likely escape route. The trunk was found largely dry, showing that it had retained a large air pocket that caused the car's tilted position in the water. That position, in turn, had allowed the tidal flow to reorient and move the car during the night and early morning.

The conditions of the car and Mary Jo's body reveal much about the truthfulness of Kennedy's statement. His companion, sitting in the front passenger seat, was thrown violently against the right front door and window and then against the ceiling, as the car struck the water first on its right side and then its roof. Upon impact, shards of sharp, tempered glass from her shattered side window struck her head, shoulder, and right arm. There were no restraining seatbelts. Lacerations, abrasions, and contusions on the face, head, arm, and shoulder seem inevitable for a front passenger-seat occupant. But there were no such injuries whatsoever to Mary Jo! With Kennedy's companion sitting with him in the front seat as observed by Deputy Look and later testified to by Kennedy, we can conclude beyond a shadow of a doubt that *Mary Jo was not the companion in the front seat.*

In an interview for the *Investigative Reports: Chappaquiddick* television program, Robert A. Dubois, a crash expert, concurred strongly with this conclusion, stating, "I would expect the passenger on the right-hand side would exhibit considerable evidence of injuries. . . . The lack of any evidence to the skin of injuries is simply amazing to me. . . . [Mary Jo in] the right front seat doesn't seem to make sense to me at all."

Mary Jo's body being found in the rear-seat compartment, with no injuries caused by the shattered window, is completely consistent with her having been lying down in the backseat, with her feet toward the right side. As the forward momentum of the car was brought to a halt by successive impacts with the water, the inertia of the front-seat passenger's body would have carried it forward within the car, throwing it against the right door and window and then the ceiling as the car hit the water on its right side and then its roof. There is no tendency for a body to move from the front seat to backseat during such an impact. Also, getting from the front seat to the backseat after the crash in the flooded, upside-down car would have required diving downward to get under the inverted seatback, an unlikely maneuver when exit through the smashed-out passenger-side window or the open driver's window was available. Thus, every bit of evidence supports Mary Jo being in the rear seat at the time of the crash.

Of course, the Kennedy team realized the problem of Mary Jo's body being found in the rear-seat compartment, an unlikely location for the only passenger he claimed was in the car. So Arthur D. Little, a Cambridge, Massachusetts, management and technology consulting firm, was hired to recreate the crash with a dummy in the front passenger seat. The result was that the dummy was "partially"[8] in the backseat after the crash, but what that meant is problematic. It is certainly far from an explicit finding that the front-seat dummy was thrown to the rear compartment.

Mary Jo's body being in the rear seat is also consistent with her leaving the party to sleep off too much to drink on the backseat of the roomy Olds 88. And Deputy Look thought he briefly caught a glimpse of a person in the backseat of the car at the Dike and Chappaquiddick roads intersection, as the car came to a halt, jerked backward, and then zoomed forward down Dike Road.

Of course, one of the most puzzling questions is why Mary Jo was not noticed asleep on the rear seat, by either Kennedy or his front-seat companion. Probably the most important factor in this unfortunate oversight was their impaired perception from an evening of heavy drinking. One's focus becomes narrowed from substantial intake of alcohol. Kennedy's inability to see and react to the approaching Dike Bridge is certainly proof of this. Also, when he and his companion entered the darkened car, the moon had already sunk below the horizon, and the angle of the lamppost light in the yard would not have illuminated the backseat.

Why Mary Jo was unable to get out through the completely blown-out rear side window will never be known, but imagining the situation helps to understand it. She was asleep and groggy from far more alcohol than she was used to drinking. Suddenly there was the shock of the car striking the water on its right side, then bouncing onto its top, throwing Mary Jo down to the ceiling.

The lack of any visible injuries or even blemishes on her body suggests that her feet were toward or against the right side of the car, which hit the water first. She was shocked awake, dazed and disoriented by the car overturning and terrified as water poured through the broken and open windows enveloping her. The weight of the engine pulled the front of the car down, causing the front-seat compartment to fill with water first. The water level rose quickly in the backseat compartment, with some air being trapped initially in the backseat foot wells of the overturned car. Instinctively, Mary Jo would have struggled to raise her head above the surface of the rising water and into the trapped pocket of air. The pocket could initially have been a foot or so high, but the ruptured seal of the crushed-in, rear, passenger-side door would have let the air slowly bubble out, shrinking the pocket. She grasped the edge of the seat with the strength of eagle's talons in order to hold her cocked-back head and finally just her nose in the vanishing air pocket. The headlights remained on for a time, producing a glow in the murky water that faded as the salt water soon drained the battery. Then it was pitch black in the water at that moonless time of night. From a foggy sleep, Mary Jo would have taken many moments to come to her senses, grasp the strange situation, and comprehend her predicament. Then she may have tried to exit the rear driver-side door or window that was initially near her head. But the car was upside down, and the water level had quickly risen well above the closed, inverted left window as well as the shattered right window. The window and door handles were under water, upside down, and unfamiliar to her. She must have tried frantically to operate them. One can imagine Mary Jo's successive feelings of terror as she was engulfed in water, momentary relief as she found the air pocket, frenzy as she searched for a way out, anxiety as rescue did not materialize, hope as she prayed fervently, and finally helplessness, tense resignation, and agony as she lived out her last tragic minutes.

How long she lived, breathing in that air pocket, engendered a controversy that persists to this day, as some believe it could have been even an hour. Whether she exhausted the air pocket of oxygen and suffocated, or inhaled water and drowned, or quite possibly died from a combination of both remains unresolved by the cursory medical examination and lack of an autopsy. The body's buoyancy and the little water that drained from the lungs suggest that suffocation at least played a role.

What if Kennedy and his companion had immediately reported the accident to the police, with the help of Mrs. Malm at Dyke House? The police would have come and been told that everyone got out of the car, since neither Kennedy nor his companion knew that Mary Jo was in it. The police would have said they would call a wrecker to recover the car in the morning. The real tragedy — Mary Jo's death — would not have been averted. But the wrecking of Kennedy's presidential ambition might have been avoided. As it happened, it was his dishonesty that wrecked that.

Since the length of time that Mary Jo survived in the car was unimportant to her possible rescue, as concluded here, deciding between drowning and suffocation as the cause of death becomes far less important than many writers have thought.

Of course, in Kennedy's concocted story of Mary Jo being a known occupant in the car, she *might* have been saved if the crash had been reported immediately. Water-rescue expert Farrar stated many times that, if immediately called, he could have brought Mary Jo up within three-quarters of an hour of being notified, and he believed that the air bubble in the rear foot well could have sustained her for at least that long. *Thus, in Kennedy's fabricated new story, ironically, he was far more culpable in Mary Jo's death than in reality!*

Chapter 5

The Aftermath

It was now past noon on Saturday in the Edgartown police headquarters on upper Main Street. Chief Arena had typed Kennedy's statement, which Kennedy had dictated to Markham, but had forgotten to ask Kennedy to sign it. Though it contained obvious peculiarities that invited queries, he made no attempt to question Kennedy further. When Kennedy requested that the statement be withheld from the press until he had conferred with his lawyer, Burke Marshall, Arena readily agreed, accepting Markham's assurance that Kennedy would then be willing to answer questions. At the time, Arena was sure that meant later in the afternoon.

Arena thought he could treat the whole incident as simply a motor vehicle accident, so he needed Kennedy's driver's license number and its expiration date in order to fill out the accident report. But Kennedy did not have his license, a violation of law that was never pursued by the authorities. He thought it might be in his other car in Washington, so he put in a call to David Burke at his Washington office to search for it. But by the end of the day it had not been found. (Interestingly, when Kennedy was ticketed for speeding in Duxbury, Massachusetts, in 1986, he once again failed to have his driver's license with him and, that time, was fined appropriately.[1])

Before Kennedy could leave the police station, Inspector George Kennedy of the Motor Vehicle Registry and his assistant, Robert Molla, needed to interview him. The missing license was again an issue, as was the automobile registration that Kennedy thought must still be in the vehicle (which it was). After reading Kennedy's statement, the inspector began to ask questions about it. Kennedy, who had been under increasing tension as the hours passed, snapped that he would make no further comments, ending the interview.

Kennedy was anxious to get off the island and home to Hyannis Port, and the sooner the better. When Markham's attempt to charter a light plane met with no success, Arena offered to call a pilot he knew who owned an airplane. When a flight to Hyannis was arranged, Arena got Molla to drive Kennedy, Markham, and Gargan to the airport. To top it off, Arena then helped them sneak out the back door into Molla's car, almost unnoticed by the horde of reporters that was already milling around the front door of the police headquarters. Kennedy's escape from questioning was complete.

In the short ride to Martha's Vineyard Airport, Kennedy's tension, bottled up throughout the morning, began to spill out. "Oh my God, what has happened? What's happened?" he moaned in frustration and regret.[2] Contrast this state of mind to his demeanor at 7:30 A.M. that day, when he chatted, relaxed and amiable, on the deck of his room. The drastic change in his manner makes it crystal clear that he was totally unaware of Mary Jo's death before Gargan and Markham's arrival at his room. He simply could not have had that casual and carefree morning demeanor if he had known he had abandoned Mary Jo to drown, as his now anxious afternoon demeanor makes obvious. In the morning, he thought his mere one-car, unobserved accident with no injuries had been "taken care of." Now, his dishonest handling of that had entrapped him in much deeper trouble. For the moment, at least, he was shattered.

With Kennedy gone, Arena retreated to his office to take stock of his investigation. One loose end he needed to tie up was finding out the full and correctly spelled name of the Mary Something in Kennedy's statement. That Katama Shores room key found in Rosemary Keough's handbag in Kennedy's car came to mind. Perhaps a second call to the inn would locate her. He gave it a try. This time she answered.

When Arena introduced himself as the Edgartown police chief, he detected a nervous wariness and quaver in Keough's voice.[3] She covered the phone to hold a muffled conversation — longer than needed to get the spelling that she must have known anyway — before giving the spelling of "Kopechne." She then requested the return of her handbag, showing her awareness of the earlier call concerning it. When Arena agreed, she, likely not wanting to be seen or interrogated, said someone would pick it up for her. Missing a chance to see and question her, Arena consented to that also. When a man appeared just a few minutes later, Arena gave him the handbag — the one piece of evidence he had — without even asking his identity!

Missed opportunity? Yes. How could Arena, based on what he knew at that time, not ask Keough on the phone about the following: How did her handbag get into Kennedy's car? Had she been in the car when it went into Poucha Pond? How was she acquainted with Kennedy or Mary Jo? What had the six young women been doing Friday night when they failed to sleep in their rooms at the motel? Almost any answer to these obvious questions — obvious, it would seem, to the investigator of a fatal accident that was as suspiciously described as in Kennedy's statement — would have revealed the Chappaquiddick cottage party. It would have then been natural for him to arrange interviews at that time with the five women at Katama. How that would have changed the course of events!

Imagine what he might have found out. One of the five, Keough as suggested by the present account, would likely have had bruises on her head and cuts and scratches on her face and right arm, called "dicing," from the implosion of the passenger-side, tempered-glass, car window. Arena might then have asked the boiler-room gals the times when Kennedy left and returned to the cottage. Was anyone with him then? Where was Mary Jo? What was said at that time? What if one or more of the boiler-room girls had refused to answer questions or insisted on consulting an attorney first? That could have set off alarm bells about the truthfulness of Kennedy's statement. Missed opportunity? Definitely yes.

A while after Arena hung up, he began to put two and two together: maybe Keough knew something about the accident. He called back to the motel. But in that short time, she and the other four young women had checked out. Gargan, still on the island on a damage-control assignment, had told Tretter, who was the man who picked up the handbag immediately, to get the young women to the ferry and off the island quickly. One can wish that Arena had had the panache of many a TV detective to jump in his cruiser and head for the Vineyard Haven ferry terminal to intercept the young women for questioning before they left.

Then Arena remembered seeing Crimmins around the police headquarters early in the afternoon, but when he looked around for him to question, he was gone too. So before the afternoon was over, the entire cookout crowd had fled the island, and Arena had not posed a single question of substance to any one of them!

There still was one aspect of the Kennedy damage-control operation that was unfinished: get Mary Jo's body off the island and into the control of her parents for funeral and burial arrangements. That was Dun Gifford's assignment. Though he had quickly obtained the Kopechnes' authorization to have the body taken to Pennsylvania, he, nonetheless, had no power to implement this unilaterally. But he was a smooth, low-key, and effective facilitator. When he enquired about the need for an autopsy, he learned that none was being recommended by Mills or the district attorney's office but that the issue was still under discussion. He visited Eugene Frieh's mortuary, diplomatically pressed for executing a death certificate and other paperwork, and then, with Frieh's assistant, Guay, took the certificate to Mills's office Saturday afternoon for his signature, all with an air of just wishing to help expedite matters.

The issue of a need for an autopsy was a "hot potato" tossed gingerly from one official to another all that afternoon, each aware of the national limelight that was beginning to glare on them, each aware of the minimum requirement of his office, and each aware of the possible political fallout on his future career. Not surprisingly, none who had the power to do so was willing to make the decision unilaterally. As the phone calls passed between the relevant officials, each expressed his argument for why an autopsy was not needed, but each left it to the other official to make the firm decision. Mills regarded the death as an obvious case of drowning, from his short examination of the body at the accident scene and from the circumstance of its recovery. Further, he had handled many drownings over the years and had never felt that an autopsy was needed. In his required reporting of the death to the district attorney's office in New Bedford, Mills made his thinking clear but indicated he would readily agree to an autopsy if the district attorney for the Southern District of Massachusetts, Edmund S. Dinis, wanted one. Dinis was not available that Saturday afternoon, so his chief investigative assistant, Detective Lieutenant George Killen of the state police, told Mills none was needed if he was satisfied with his finding of the cause of death. When Dinis, politically ambitious with a reelection bid just a year away, became aware of the Kennedy case, he wanted no part of it. Using the excuse that his office seldom, if ever, prosecuted automobile accident cases, he was happy to leave the responsibility in Mills's hands. However, he later claimed he had changed his mind on the Sunday morning following the accident, had called Killen to have an autopsy performed, but was told (erroneously) that the body had already been flown to Pennsylvania.

Arena, who had shown deference to Kennedy throughout their interaction, was reluctant to charge him with any crime. He patiently waited for the further statement from Kennedy, as Markham had promised, expecting it would be adequately exculpatory. But as the Saturday afternoon wore on, it became apparent to Arena that there would be no further statement coming from Kennedy. With a horde of reporters pressuring him for more information, Arena decided to release it. But he continued to resist charging Kennedy with anything.

"As late as 5 p.m. on Saturday Chief Arena said that he would not bring charges against the senator," reported the *Vineyard Gazette*.[4] But under the glare of publicity and realizing that the nine-hour delay in reporting a fatal accident could not be ignored, Arena announced late that evening that he would bring a misdemeanor complaint of leaving the scene of an accident. On sober reflection, he realized he had to do that much based just on Kennedy's own written admission. But he was aiming at nothing more than a citation for that. In Arena's thinking, the death was simply an accidental drowning that needed no autopsy. This thinking ignored the possibility of a manslaughter charge, required by Massachusetts law if the driver left the scene of a fatal accident in which he was believed to be negligent. Then an autopsy would be very important to the prosecution. And it would seem that any reasonable interpretation of the law would regard driving off a bridge as negligent, if not reckless.

With those thoughts running through his mind, Arena felt that the hot potato was in his hands, so he conferred with Walter Steele, the special prosecutor for the Dukes County District Court. Steele, a young man with blonde hair, a narrow face, and large glasses, was a recent Democratic appointee and would later be appointed the judge of that court. He took an ambiguous stance, suggesting, "When in doubt, do an autopsy,"[5] but also telling Arena that they had done all that was required of them, that is, notifying the district attorney's office of the possible need for an autopsy. Steele bobbled the hot potato too.

Steele admitted on the *Investigative Reports* program years later that political implications were constantly evaluated: "I was not going to participate in any unjust assault on Kennedy because I'm a Democrat."[6] Not surprisingly, given that attitude, Steele was happy to concur with Arena that there was no negligence in the accident and so no adequately strong case for manslaughter and, therefore, no need for an autopsy. Not surprisingly also, with all this avoidance thinking circulating among the officials, Mills felt free to release the body late in the day for embalming by Frieh.

Ten years after the accident, Steele mused, "I really should have known better. If I had it to do over again, I would have held out for a probable cause hearing for manslaughter and an autopsy."[7] Of course, if he had "known better," he likely would not have been appointed a judge later. Of all the participants in the aftermath of the Chappaquiddick tragedy, Steele at least leads in the honesty of his self-evaluation.

While the autopsy hot potato was being tossed between the law-enforcement personnel, mortician Frieh had transported the body to his funeral home and begun cleansing it for burial. He made a further examination for trauma, finding none unless a slight abrasion of a left knuckle were counted. The relatively small amount of water that was expelled from the body at the accident scene and at his mortuary led Frieh to wonder whether suffocation was a more likely cause of death than drowning. So, being cautious, he wisely delayed embalming in case Mills or Killen or Dinis or Arena or Steele were to change his mind.

Frieh personally thought there should be an autopsy "for three reasons: the type of accident it was; the important people involved; and the fact that insurance companies would be hounding officials over double indemnity claims,"[8] but he was not in the decision loop.

As Frieh awaited a decision on an autopsy, he realized he needed instructions on where to ship the body if none were to be performed. Late that Saturday afternoon, all the necessary information came in a telephone call from the Kielty Funeral Home of Plymouth, Pennsylvania, which was hired by the Kopechne family to handle funeral and burial arrangements, apparently facilitated by Gifford's smooth interventions. With no official autopsy hold forthcoming, Frieh proceeded to oversee Guay do the embalming.

Gifford's assignment also included escorting Mary Jo's remains on a flight paid for by Kennedy to Pennsylvania. The plane was scheduled to depart Martha's Vineyard Airport on Sunday morning, but an equipment problem forced a change of planes and delayed departure until shortly after noon. Dinis would later testify at an exhumation and autopsy hearing that he had changed his mind in favor of an autopsy, had informed his assistant Killen of his change of mind during the aircraft delay, but was told erroneously that the plane had departed for Pennsylvania. Some were skeptical of the claim.

As Arena's thinking about charging Kennedy slowly changed late Saturday, he realized he needed the senator's driver's license, which he had not furnished. Arena needed confirmation that Kennedy had a license, and he needed its expiration date to complete the motor vehicle accident report. At the end of the day, he called the Motor Vehicle Registry Office to obtain this information, but no valid license could be found. The only record there indicated that Kennedy's license had expired earlier that year, on February 22. This was made known to several registry officials on Sunday, and — surprise! — on Monday morning, a valid license was found mysteriously in an irregular location in the office. Needless to say, political shenanigans have been charged and may well have occurred. But the result was that the required information was delivered to Arena that morning. He then completed his motor vehicle accident report.

Arena, who had been helpful to Kennedy throughout his ordeal, now did him the greatest favor of all: he absolved him of negligence and, to the extent that he could, so removed a possible involuntary manslaughter or even a driving-to-endanger charge from consideration. In the accident report, Arena concluded, "It was felt that because of the evidence at the scene, condition of the roadway and accident scene that there was no negligence on the part of the operator in the accident."[9] Think about it. This law-enforcement officer concluded — and then repeatedly defended — that driving off a bridge is just normal, competent driving! Or at least it should be for a senator.

Arena then obtained court authorization to issue a complaint against Kennedy for leaving the scene of an accident. Kennedy's Edgartown lawyer, Richard McCarron, immediately requested a hearing. The court scheduled it for the following Monday, July 28.

Now, with an opportunity for Steele to examine and cross-examine witnesses scheduled, Arena suddenly realized that he had to get his investigation out of idling and into high gear. He gathered statements from the Shiretown Inn manager, Russell Peachey; front-desk clerk Frances Stewart; Sylvia Malm at Dyke House; and Deputy Look. Jack Crimmins indicated a willingness to speak to Arena, so they arranged a meeting off-island in Falmouth, Cape Cod. Again Arena was happy with the offer of a written statement and again he did not ask a single question after reading the statement, which added nothing of substance to the investigation. Crimmins's main point seemed to be characterizing the Chappaquiddick party as just a quiet cookout, far from the noisy, inebriated hilarity described by the neighboring Silvas.

Over the weekend, hordes of reporters flocked to Martha's Vineyard to feed the growing curiosity of a national audience. Their badgering for the latest developments led Arena at the beginning of the week to start twice-daily press briefings in the parish house of the Federated Church. This traditional New England-style church, whose congregation dates from 1642, was conveniently located near the center of Edgartown. For support and occasional guidance on what or how much to say, Arena had Steele at his side. Soon a wag dubbed these briefings "The Dominick and Walter Show."[10] But Arena's investigation was not finding enough to fill the time, so the church's need for the space for its annual Whale of a Sale[11] became a good reason to end the regular press briefings on Thursday. When this last source of news dried up, one waggish reporter wrote, "The newsmen stood around on the church lawn again and resumed interviewing each other."[12]

Meanwhile, Joseph and Gwen Kopechne had a requiem mass held for their daughter, Mary Jo, on Tuesday at St. Vincent's Roman Catholic Church, located in Plymouth in central Pennsylvania, after which she was laid to rest in the parish cemetery atop Larksville Mountain. Kennedy and his wife, Joan, as well as Gargan and the remaining boiler-room gals, attended.

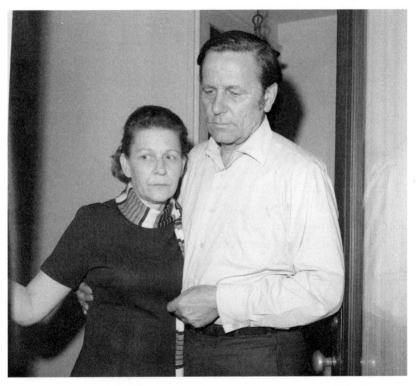

Gwen and Joseph Kopechne, parents of Mary Jo (© Bettmann/CORBIS)

Gifford, who had returned there on Monday as a sort of advance man for Kennedy, was in the good graces of the Kopechnes and acted as one of the pallbearers. With his offer to be as helpful as possible to the Kopechnes during all the distressing commotion, Gifford had managed to insinuate himself into a position where "he manipulated all the information supplied to Gwen and Joe relating to the accident,"[13] as reported by Jerry Shaffer and Leslie H. Leland in their recent book, *Left to Die*. Gifford's smoothness in this role was so complete that, years later, Joe was effusive in praising him: "Dun Gifford was very kind and generous, he helped us a lot. He let us answer our phone. He never made any suggestions one way or another as to how we should handle ourselves. You have to respect somebody like that, because he was a Kennedy man."[14] But still later, after a much delayed visit of inquiry to Martha's Vineyard, Joe's thoughts had reversed: "They [Kennedy people] never told us the truth and they wouldn't let us talk with anyone who could provide accurate information. They manipulated us."[15]

During the week following the wreck, a cadre of advisors gathered at the Kennedy compound in Hyannis Port to combine their expertise in law, politics, and public relations to formulate the strategy for Kennedy's defense. Stephen Smith, Kennedy's brother-in-law, managed the group. Interestingly, Kennedy himself was but a bit player, remaining quite withdrawn and uncommunicative. Whether he "came clean" with his inner circle is not known. Among the many advisors were Ted Sorensen, the speechwriter; Robert McNamara, the defense secretary; and Richard Goodwin, also a speechwriter, all from Jack Kennedy's administration. Also participating in the councils were Milton Gwirtzman, a speechwriter for Ted Kennedy, and a team of legal experts: Burke Marshall, who had served under Bobby Kennedy in the Justice Department; Edward B. Hanify, a prominent Boston attorney; Robert G. Clark, Jr., an expert motor vehicle litigator of Brockton, Massachusetts, and former district court judge; and Richard McCarron, an Edgartown attorney with desirable local knowledge and connections, including being the town counsel. Gargan was there also but was mostly ignored.

In the days following the accident, the lack of an autopsy continued to cause public speculation, some rather lurid, about what it might reveal. The question was given official backing when Medical Examiner Dr. Robert Nevin, who had been off-duty when Assistant Medical Examiner Mills handled the case, publicly endorsed an autopsy. Nevin said that it could put to rest a lot of shabby rumors and that embalming would not hinder determining the cause of death. He openly criticized his colleague for not calling for an autopsy when Mills became aware of all the circumstances on Saturday afternoon, particularly the prominence of the person involved and the likely publicity that would ensue. Later, Nevin made his criticism more personal by calling Mills "a sweet, gentle, kind person" who "would not take a stand unless pushed."[16] Mills fired back in kind.

Also during the week, a strange meeting occurred that puts both Arena and Steele in a much less favorable light.[17] Arena's deference to Kennedy had been on display all week. Steele, though less in the limelight, had concurred with Arena's handling of the case. This meeting showed that they were both willing to go further than that to protect Kennedy, to the extent of trying to influence the grand jury to take no action. Leslie H. Leland, a twenty-nine-year-old pharmacist just getting Leslie's Drug Store in Vineyard Haven under way, was the foreman of the grand jury. At the time, he was not aware of the independent powers of investigation endowed in a grand jury. He thought that the prosecutor had all the investigative authority and capability, while the grand jury's role was simply to judge whether the prosecutor's evidence was sufficient to bring the accused to trial. Steele and Arena, aware that a grand jury could initiate its own investigation through its subpoena power, apparently were worried that it might exercise that power on the Chappaquiddick accident, because they realized that District Attorney Dinis wished to avoid involvement.

When Arena called Leland for a meeting, Leland did not know what it would be about and was puzzled by Arena's desire for privacy — or was it secrecy? He agreed to meet Arena at the Blinker Light, the only traffic signal then on the island (except for one at the Lagoon drawbridge), now replaced by a roundabout. There Leland was picked up by an unmarked car driven by Arena, with Steele in the front passenger seat. Then the strangeness began: neither Arena nor Steele spoke to Leland in the rear seat, only to each other, as they drove around a long loop of roads. The substance of the conversation between the two was that Kennedy's Chappaquiddick accident had been thoroughly investigated, it had been determined to be a minor traffic violation, and there was no need for further investigation, certainly not any by the grand jury. With those points made emphatically, but indirectly, to Leland, they returned to the Blinker and dropped him off. He was left amazed and confused but especially intimidated.

By the middle of the week, the Kennedy strategy team had decided on a course of action. There were a number of considerations that had to be balanced. They did not want a hearing where all of those at the Chappaquiddick party could be subpoenaed to testify and then cross-examined. That offered many uncertainties and dangers, and there was little time to prepare. The complaint filed against Kennedy was only for leaving the scene of an accident in which bodily injury had occurred and failing to report it in a timely manner. The registry had just announced that Kennedy's driver's license had been suspended, as required by law, with a preliminary finding of negligence on his part, a finding that tended to nullify Arena's accommodating opinion. That brought up thoughts of a worst-case scenario — a charge of involuntary manslaughter. So the best course of action, the Kennedy strategists concluded, was to waive the hearing and have Kennedy plead guilty to the charge of leaving the scene of the accident, after, of course, negotiation with the prosecution about its procedure and recommended sentence.

Judge Clark, as he was still called, was the Kennedy team negotiator who came to Edgartown on Wednesday evening for an initial meeting with Steele and Arena. Clark made it clear that decisions were being made in Hyannis Port and the meeting was only exploratory. He was pleased with what he heard and, after consultations back in Hyannis Port, flew into the island again on Thursday afternoon for a second meeting that was held at the Martha's Vineyard Airport, away from the hordes of reporters. To Arena's surprise, Clark said that Kennedy wished to waive the hearing and plead guilty to leaving the scene. From Arena and Steele's point of view, this would be a fine outcome. It would show the public that they had done something and show the Democratic politicos and the Kennedy aficionados that they had done the minimum. And little effort from them would be required. Of course, they could not predict what Judge Boyle of the district court would do. Boyle, who had spent twenty-seven years as the clerk of the Dukes County Superior Court before his judicial appointment in 1961, was generally regarded as a fair judge but not a particularly sharp intellect. The Massachusetts statute mandated a minimum sentence of two months in jail. Clark wanted to know what sentence Steele would recommend and whether he would be willing to recommend that it be suspended. Yes, two months and suspended would be fine with him. The feeling was that Boyle would go along with such a recommendation.

Clark, not wanting any surprises, asked Arena what statement he would make to the court. Arena obligingly typed out a simple summary of the facts and showed it to Clark, who found it completely acceptable. For reasons left unsaid, Clark did not want to wait until Monday, when the hearing was scheduled. Would not Judge Boyle agree to move it up to Friday morning? That took some quick checking. Luckily there was nothing on the docket for Friday, and at the request of Steele, Boyle agreed to hear the case at 9:00 A.M. At their meeting, Steele most likely briefed Boyle on the expected plea, Arena's statement, and his own recommendations of the minimum two-month sentence and its suspension.

It was then already the middle of Thursday evening, and Arena did not want the early Friday-morning court session to appear as an attempt to avoid public scrutiny. In fact, he wanted publicity for obtaining a conviction as closure to the case. So he had his officers spread the word informally to the numerous reporters staying in Edgartown. Next Arena, mindful of the two previous Kennedy assassinations and all the negative publicity that Ted Kennedy was then receiving, arranged security for Kennedy while on the island.

The next morning, Kennedy, accompanied by his wife, Joan, and Stephen Smith, arrived on the Kennedy yacht *Marlin* in the pocket harbor of Oak Bluffs and were driven five miles with a police escort to the 112-year-old, red brick courthouse on Main Street in Edgartown. With the district court in session, the clerk, Tommy Teller, read the complaint and asked Kennedy how he would plead. In a weak and emotional voice came the reply, "Guilty." At Judge Boyle's request, Arena then read his short, prepared statement. Next Boyle, directing a question at "the defendant or the Commonwealth,"[18] asked whether Kennedy had deliberately attempted to conceal his identity after the accident, clearly wondering about Kennedy's fleeing Chappaquiddick to Edgartown. Arena, unprepared for such a question, stammered, "Not to my knowledge." Steele then chimed in his concurrence with Arena. Kennedy, happy to have the Commonwealth protecting him, remained silent. Boyle, apparently realizing that what he might learn in pressing the question further could force his hand in the sentencing, abandoned the inquiry without obtaining an answer from Kennedy.

When local defense attorney McCarron then tried to make a statement of possible legal defenses that Kennedy could have used (and possibly some exculpatory remarks), Judge Boyle cut him off as being out of order after a guilty plea. McCarron then asked that any sentence the judge chose to impose be suspended, based on Kennedy's reputation and character. Prosecutor Steele then recommended the minimum sentence of two months in the Barnstable House of Correction, but suspended, and a year of probation. Boyle enquired of the probation officer whether Kennedy had any record of serious driving offences. Receiving an answer of "none," Boyle stated, "Where it is my understanding, he has already been and will continue to be punished far beyond anything this court can impose — the ends of justice would be satisfied by the imposition of the minimum jail sentence and the suspension of that sentence, assuming the defendant accepts the suspension."[19] That seems specious: actual jail time has an impact on the guilty person and on public opinion of the crime far beyond a suspended sentence. McCarron quickly agreed to the suspension, a necessary legal procedure that gives up the right of appeal.[20] That zero jail time is not less than the minimum two-month jail time required by law is a mathematical quirk of the legal mind. Kennedy's guilty plea under Massachusetts law also led to an automatic driver's-license suspension for one year.

Had the probation officer not attested to a clean driving record for Kennedy, a minimum sentence would have been unlikely and a suspension of it highly unlikely. Was it that clean? This is a very debatable issue. Kennedy had been convicted of three moving violations while attending the University of Virginia Law School from 1957 to 1959.[21] These involved speeding, running red lights, driving without an operator's license, and attempting to elude arrest. These transgressions, which go unmentioned in his memoir,[22] seem quite consonant with his expulsion from Harvard for a year for cheating on an exam. In one of the traffic cases where he was convicted of all charges at trial, the arresting officer had cited him for "reckless driving; racing with an officer to avoid arrest; operating a motor vehicle without an operator's license."[23] His attempt to "avoid arrest" is particularly noteworthy in light of his fleeing to Edgartown following the Chappaquiddick accident. It is not known whether Massachusetts authorities knew of these offences, but if they did, the occurrences more than six years previous would not, under Massachusetts law, have prevented his record from being regarded legally as "clean."

Interestingly, these traffic violations were discovered by a reporter in Charlottesville, Virginia, at just that time and were circulated by the Associated Press on the Friday Kennedy pled guilty.[24] If the hearing had occurred on the following Monday, as originally scheduled, Kennedy's early history of serious moving violations would have been nationally known before his trial and sentencing. Would the result have been the same? Quite possibly not. Had Clark's insistence on moving up the hearing resulted from the Kennedy camp somehow learning that this damaging information was about to become public knowledge?

Kennedy's court appearance had been choreographed with the expertise of a Balanchine ballet, and everyone had danced their parts flawlessly. Not a single new fact about the Dike Bridge crash or Mary Jo's death had been revealed. Kennedy had not answered any question other than his plea. He was now free to massage his story further.

As he left the courthouse, he announced from its front steps to a throng of waiting reporters that he had requested time on the three national television networks that evening to explain the tragedy to his Massachusetts electorate and the nation.

The massaging was about to begin.

Chapter 6

The Television Speech

Apart from attending the Kopechne funeral, Kennedy remained secluded in the family compound in Hyannis Port during the entire week following the accident. He avoided answering any questions by the authorities and did not utter a single word of explanation publicly. Instead, he gathered a battery of counselors — attorneys, speechwriters, and public-relations advisors — to prepare the statement that the public was awaiting and demanding. The public's thirst for information had grown by the day. Reporters, cameramen, and columnists had been left to do their own detective work and churn out copy, much of it speculative and almost all of it critical. The Kennedys had always been very open with the press, cultivating a good-natured relationship that helped advance their several political careers. This time, rather than easy access, the press experienced total exclusion. That alone enhanced suspicions. That alone suggested there was much to hide. But now Kennedy was going to tell the whole story on television — or was he?

The Chappaquiddick accident had become such a newsworthy event — at times even pushing aside Neil Armstrong's historic first walk on the moon — that all three major television networks of the time, ABC, CBS, and NBC, gave Kennedy a fifteen-minute, live, public-interest, prime-time slot at 7:30 P.M. for his address. Kennedy, seated at a desk in the Hyannis Port family home, read from a manuscript carefully prepared by his team of writers and advisors:

My fellow citizens, I have requested this opportunity to talk to you, the people of Massachusetts, about the tragedy which happened last Friday evening.

This morning I entered a plea of guilty to the charge of leaving the scene of an accident. Prior to my appearance in court it would have been improper for me to comment on these matters, but tonight I am free to tell you what happened and to say what it means to me.

On the weekend of July 18th, I was on Martha's Vineyard Island participating with my nephew, Joe Kennedy, as for thirty years my family has participated in the annual Edgartown Sailing Regatta. Only reasons of health prevented my wife from accompanying me.

On Chappaquiddick Island off Martha's Vineyard, I attended on Friday evening, July 18th, a cookout I had encouraged and helped sponsor for a devoted group of Kennedy campaign secretaries. When I left the party around 11:15 P.M., I was accompanied by one of these girls, Miss Mary Jo Kopechne. Mary Jo was one of the most devoted members of the staff of Senator Robert Kennedy. She worked for him for four years and was broken up over his death. For this reason and because she was such a gentle, kind, and idealistic person, all of us tried to help her feel that she was still at home with the Kennedy family.

There is no truth whatever to the widely circulated suspicions of immoral conduct that have been leveled at my behavior and hers regarding that evening. There never has been a private relationship between us of any kind. I know of nothing in Mary Jo's conduct on that or any other occasion — and the same is true of the other girls at that party — that would lend any substance to such ugly speculation about their character. Nor was I driving under the influence of liquor.

Little over a mile away the car that I was driving on an unlit road went off a narrow bridge which had no guard rails and was built on a left angle to the road. The car overturned into a deep pond and immediately filled with water. I remember thinking as the cold water rushed in around my head, that I was for certain drowning; then water entered my lungs and I actually felt the sensation of drowning; but somehow I struggled to the surface alive. I made immediate and repeated efforts to save Mary Jo by diving into the strong and murky current, but succeeded only in increasing my state of utter exhaustion and alarm.

My conduct and conversation during the next several hours, to the extent that I can remember them, made no sense to me at all. Although my doctors inform me that I received a cerebral concussion as well as shock, I do not seek to escape responsibility for my actions by placing the blame either on the physical and emotional trauma brought on by the accident, or on anyone else. I regard as indefensible the fact that I did not report the accident to the police immediately. Instead of looking directly for a telephone after lying exhausted on the grass for an undetermined time, I walked back to the cottage where the party was being held, requested the help of two friends, Joe Gargan and Paul Markham, and directed them to return immediately to the scene with me (it then being sometime after midnight) in order to undertake a new effort to dive down and locate Miss Kopechne. Their strenuous efforts, undertaken at some risk to their own lives, also proved futile.

All kinds of scrambled thoughts — all of them confused, some of them irrational, many of which I cannot recall, and some of which I would not have seriously entertained under normal circumstances — went through my mind during this period. They were reflected in the various inexplicable, inconsistent, and inconclusive things I said and did — including such questions as whether the girl might still be alive somewhere out of the immediate area, whether some awful curse actually did hang over all the Kennedys, whether there was some justifiable reason for me to doubt what had happened and to delay my report, and whether somehow the awful weight of this incredible incident might in some way pass from my shoulders. I was overcome, I am frank to say, by a jumble of emotions — grief, fear, doubt, exhaustion, panic, confusion, and shock.

Instructing Gargan and Markham not to alarm Mary Jo's friends that night, I had them take me to the ferry crossing. The ferry having shut down for the night, I suddenly jumped into the water and impulsively swam across, nearly drowning once again in the effort, returning to my hotel around 2 A.M. and collapsed in my room. I remember going out at one point and saying something to the room clerk. In the morning with my mind somewhat more lucid, I made an effort to call a family legal advisor, Burke Marshall, from a public telephone on the Chappaquiddick side of the ferry, and then belatedly reported the accident to the Martha's Vineyard police.

Today, as mentioned, I felt morally obligated to plead guilty to the charge of leaving the scene of an accident. No words on my part can possibly express the terrible pain and suffering I feel over this tragic accident. This last week has been an agonizing one for me, and for the members of my family; and the grief we feel over the loss of a wonderful friend will remain with us the rest of our lives.

These events and the publicity and innuendo and whispers which have surrounded them, and my admission of guilt this morning, raises the question in my mind of whether my standing among the people of my state has been so impaired that I should resign my seat in the United States Senate. If at any time the citizens of Massachusetts should lack confidence in their senator's character or his ability, with or without justification, he could not, in my opinion, adequately perform his duties, and should not continue in office.

The people of this state — the state that sent John Quincy Adams, Daniel Webster, Charles Sumner, Henry Cabot Lodge, and John F. Kennedy to the United States Senate — are entitled to representation in that body by men that inspire their utmost confidence. For this reason I would understand full well why some might think it right for me to resign.

This would be a difficult decision to make. It has been seven years since my first election to the Senate. You and I share many memories. Some of them have been glorious; some have been very sad. The opportunity to work with you and serve our state has been much of what has made my life worthwhile.

And so I ask you tonight, the people of Massachusetts, to think this through with me. In facing this decision, I seek your advice and opinion. In making it, I seek your prayers, for this is a decision that I will have finally to make on my own.

It has been written:

"A man does what he must — in spite of personal consequences, in spite of obstacles and dangers and pressures — and that is the basis of all human morality. And whatever may be the sacrifices he faces if he follows his conscience — the loss of his friends, his fortune, his contentment, even the esteem of his fellow men — each man must decide for himself the course he will follow. The stories of past courage can not supply courage itself. For this each man must look into his own soul." I pray that I can have the courage to make the right decision. Whatever is decided, whatever the future holds for me, I hope I shall be able to put this most recent tragedy behind me and make some future contribution to our state and mankind whether it be in public or private life. Thank you and good night.

The reception of the television speech ranged from sympathy and belief to condemnation and outrage but mostly centered on all the questions it left unanswered. Kennedy had failed badly at fulfilling one of the purposes he began the speech with: "to tell you what happened." The speech, though over five times the length of his police report, added or altered only a few statements from that report. Though Kennedy maintained his time of leaving the cottage, he dropped any mention of his intent to drive to the ferry and of simply making a wrong turn onto Dike Road. While denying any amorous intentions and any excess alcohol intake, he now offered no explanation whatsoever of why he drove onto Dike Road.

This left a huge void in the story. Kennedy's relating of the events jumped from "when I left the party . . . " to "little over a mile away the car I was driving on an unlit road went off a narrow bridge." What were they doing? Where were they going? Why were they there? A midnight swim, perhaps? Best not to offer that: no one had brought a swimsuit to an evening cookout. No one among his creative-writing team could think of a respectable and convincing reason, so nothing was offered.

He described four new activities that were not in his police report. First, he admitted that he and Mary Jo had been at a party that Friday night, a fact uncovered and widely publicized by the press during the week, to Arena's chagrin. Kennedy's allusion in his police report to "where my friends were eating" had not been enough to alert Arena to the party's existence, resulting in his lack of interrogation of the party guests at the time. Second, Kennedy stated that upon returning to the cottage, he had directed his two friends, Gargan and Markham, to return with him to the accident site and attempt to rescue Mary Jo. Third, Kennedy said he had swum across the channel to return to Edgartown. Fourth, he admitted to talking to the room clerk outside his room at the Shiretown Inn sometime after 2:00 A.M.

Having just pled guilty to leaving the scene of an accident, he dropped his claim of having reported the accident "immediately" and now described it as "belatedly."

Given that the Kennedy team, huddled in the Hyannis Port compound, had had six days to devise this speech, it seems that any change from the police statement would have some interpretable reason. On first thought, the most surprising omission is the supposed reason for the drive, that is, to go to the ferry and return to their respective hotel rooms. That reason was originally given presumably to undermine any charge of an intended amorous adventure on the beach. In the speech, a whole paragraph is spent on denying any such intent as well as denying that he was driving under the influence of liquor, so perhaps the previous claim that Kennedy and Mary Jo were on a drive to the ferry — widely disbelieved during the preceding week — was deleted simply to remove the unbelievable and to fit the speech in the fifteen-minute time slot the networks had agreed to furnish.

Kennedy did continue to claim the 11:15 P.M. departure time of his drive, in spite of Deputy Look's reliable sighting of the car an hour and a half later. Further, Kennedy offered no activity after departing the cottage that could have explained that discrepancy in time.

The speech's omission of the claim that his abrupt turn off a paved road onto the gravel and dirt Dike Road was just a mistaken turn was probably simply because it had been so universally disbelieved. And no one could think up a believable replacement explanation.

The most interesting new claim was that Kennedy, accompanied by Gargan and Markham, went back to the bridge soon after the accident in a renewed attempt to rescue Mary Jo. In his police statement, Kennedy had said that at his arrival back at the cottage, "There was a car parked in front of the cottage and I climbed into the backseat. I then asked for someone to bring me back to Edgartown." That certainly denies by clear omission a return to the accident scene, and Markham participated in choosing that wording. Neither did Gargan make any mention of such a return that night back at the cottage or the following morning, according to Tretter in his inquest testimony the following January. He testified, "He [Gargan] explained that, as I recall, that the Senator had called he [*sic*] and Mr. Markham out of the cottage, had told them what had happened, and asked to be driven to the Edgartown Ferry."[1] But in his speech Kennedy inserted a renewed rescue effort at that time: "I walked back to the cottage where the party was being held, requested the help of two friends, Joe Gargan and Paul Markham, and directed them to return immediately to the scene with me (it then being sometime after midnight) in order to undertake a new effort to dive down and locate Miss Kopechne."

If Kennedy had been serious about a further rescue attempt at that time, why would he not ask LaRosa, to whom he first spoke back at the cottage, to aid in the attempt? LaRosa had earlier served nine years as a fireman and had been trained in all forms of rescue.[2] Gargan and Markham had no such training.

Kennedy's claimed rescue attempt is one of the most unbelievable parts of the whole speech. Who can believe that two mature men, Gargan and Markham, uninvolved in the accident, both trained as lawyers and Markham having served as U.S. attorney for Massachusetts, its top federal prosecutor, would not insist on reporting an apparently fatal accident immediately rather than going off on their own belated and amateurish rescue mission? The red light at the fire station was lit, its door unlocked, and its emergency siren switch available inside, and they had to drive past the station on their way to Dike Bridge. On the other hand, if they thought that the accident was simply an unobserved car that had driven off a bridge, with no fatalities or significant injuries, they could reasonably have decided it could be reported first thing in the morning. But the new rescue story invented for Kennedy's TV speech that went beyond his initially planned alibi entrapped them. Out of loyalty, Gargan and Markham acquiesced in silence about their supposed activity in Kennedy's new story. For that they received much deserved, harsh criticism.

There obviously were worries among the Kennedy coterie in Hyannis

Port about offering the second rescue attempt in his television speech, enough, in fact, that at least some of the boiler-room gals were prepped on its inclusion in the speech prior to it being aired. The worry must have been that one of them might express surprise in an interview about such an activity because it had never been mentioned at the time. Thus, David Hackett, who had been in charge of the boiler room in Bobby Kennedy's campaign and so was close to the girls (and at one time an expected attendee of the Chappaquiddick party), was dispatched to inform them of the upcoming speech's content, as Maryellen Lyons revealed later in her inquest testimony.[3]

Everyone who has simply added the necessary amounts of time for Kennedy's reported activities that night finds that there was no time for such an activity, and they reject the claim. A&E's *Investigative Reports,* for example, counted the time intervals as fifteen minutes attempting to rescue Mary Jo immediately following the accident (Kennedy's estimate at the later inquest); fifteen minutes lying on the grass exhausted (Kennedy's estimate); fifteen minutes walking back to the cottage (Kennedy's estimate; an underestimate by about fifteen minutes); forty-five minutes talking with Gargan and Markham at the cottage and then returning to the crash scene for a second attempt at rescue (Kennedy's estimate); ten minutes driving to the ferry and talking there in the car; ten minutes swimming the channel; fifteen minutes resting on the beach, leaning against a tree, and walking around before reaching his room; and thirty minutes drying off, collapsing on the bed, changing clothes, and encountering Shiretown Inn manager Peachey (Kennedy's estimate), for a total of two hours and thirty-five (or fifty) minutes. Basing Kennedy's emergence from the wreck at 12:50 A.M., based on Look's reliable sighting, *Investigative Reports* found that Kennedy would have been talking to Peachey at 3:25 A.M. (or later), a full hour later than Peachey's reliable report.

There simply was no time for this second rescue attempt that was first claimed in the television speech. It could not have happened. No one at the cottage ever reported or testified to seeing either Gargan or Markham soaking wet or disheveled, as they would have been after such an activity at that time of night. Nor did Gargan mention this exploit to the boiler-room gals that night upon returning to the cottage or the following morning when he was breaking the terrible news of Mary Jo's death to them. Kennedy's invention of Gargan and Markham's midnight diving was apparently a way of filling the time after his claimed earlier departure time of 11:15 P.M. and adding to his purported heroics.

The *Boston Globe* Spotlight Team spent two months in 1974 reinvestigating the Chappaquiddick tragedy. They wrote that a reliable source had "vigorously disputed other aspects of Kennedy's account, including the purported rescue attempt an hour after the accident."[4]

Gargan and Markham, as related earlier, must have visited the accident scene, dived into the water, and discovered Mary Jo's body. But that apparently occurred without Kennedy's participation and soon after daybreak.

Kennedy's claim that he swam the channel back to Edgartown was the third element in his speech that was not in his police report. Most likely this was introduced as a heroic action to divert attention from his reason for returning to Edgartown. Surprisingly, that attempt at diversion was successful, because at the later inquest he was not asked why he wished to return to Edgartown (one of a myriad of inquest lapses discussed below). Based on his new story of activities to that point, there was no reason whatsoever to go there. But it had been required by his initial scheme to escape involvement in the accident and establish an alibi. Now he was stuck with the evidence of his fleeing. If he had wanted to report the accident, there was a telephone at the Chappaquiddick ferry shed (as well as other opportunities he had already bypassed). He had fled the scene in his first scheme and now needed to divert attention from that.

The fourth new element in his speech was revealing his interaction with Peachey at 2:25 A.M. at the Shiretown Inn. Originally that was to be the key to Kennedy's alibi, but that had to be given up in his new story, so it no longer was of much importance. However, it was becoming known, so why not just acknowledge it?

The most telling characterization of the speech was expressed years later by Gargan, who knew more than he wished to reveal: "It was all made up, all of it, including thoughts and emotions"[5] — that is, it was just "lies, lies, lies, lies," as Leo Damore described it in *Investigative Reports*. Gargan partially explained his silence on what actually happened in another interview when, defending himself against criticism of his role in the affair, he said, "I wouldn't have tried to clear myself under circumstances where *I wasn't at liberty to discuss things I was privy to as a witness,* information that was nobody's business"[6] (emphasis added). Actually, it turned out to be everybody's business.

This is also a revealing comment by Gargan. Why was he not *"at liberty"* to speak the truth? Since both Gargan and Markham are attorneys, it is sometimes supposed that Kennedy invoked lawyer-client privilege to prevent either of them from disclosing post-accident advice. But that cannot require silence on observations made "as a witness." Further, Gargan repeatedly in interviews revealed some of his legal advice to Kennedy in the post-accident time, namely, to report the accident immediately. That resisted advice did nothing to improve Kennedy's image, as his attorney should be interested in doing, but it did help improve Gargan's own image. So if Kennedy did exercise lawyer-client privilege, Gargan chose to honor it only selectively.

Gargan's frank comments were made years after the accident and after he had broken with Kennedy, his relative and longtime friend. But he was too intertwined in the events to say more, to complete the story he knew much of.

The nation's curiosity about the particulars of the accident had built during the week prior to the speech, with many, maybe most, expecting a complete and satisfying explanation of all the circumstances surrounding the tragedy. That did not happen. Instead, disappointment, doubt, suspicion, and a greater demand for answers resulted. There was also a near universal opinion that a lot was being hidden. Editorial opinion was strongly negative and condemnatory.

While disclaiming any attempt "to escape responsibility for my actions by placing the blame either on the physical and emotional trauma brought on by the accident," Kennedy was quick to point out that his physicians had conveniently diagnosed him with a "cerebral concussion as well as shock." He implied that this diagnosis explained his "scrambled thoughts" and "jumble of emotions," in hopes of mitigating the crime he had just pled guilty to that morning. The diagnosis, made at least sixteen hours after the accident, contradicts Kennedy's behavior as reported by every person who came in contact with him during that interval. Gargan, who was with Kennedy soon after the accident that night, has said flatly, "He wasn't in shock at that point."[7]

While Kennedy's speech began with his account of the happenings around the Chappaquiddick accident, its concluding part was entirely a political appeal. To give the latter a more personal feel, he had set aside the script and spoken directly to the camera, using unseen flashcards. He sought sympathy for "the terrible pain and suffering" he and his family felt but made no mention of the far worse pain and suffering the parents of Mary Jo, their only child, must have felt! It is hard to imagine Kennedy and his renowned set of speechwriters being that callous, but they were so wrapped up in pushing Kennedy's story that they were. He sought forgiveness for the tragic accident while ignoring the web of lies he had spun to cover up so much about it. He sought self-elevation by citing some of the great men who had preceded him in the Massachusetts senatorial seat and quoting at length from his brother's book *Profiles in Courage*. All of that was prologue to an appeal to his constituents for support to continue as U.S. senator, under the guise that he was considering resignation. That sealed the speech as simply a political ploy, not the hoped-for explanation that could put people's minds at rest.

Chapter 7

The Autopsy Hearing

Kennedy's speech was a booming success at the purpose for which it was designed: mustering political support among his devoted Massachusetts constituency. Tens of thousands of telegrams — then the only method of rapid, written communication — poured in to the Hyannis Port compound. Staff members claimed that the telegrams were a hundred to one in favor of Kennedy retaining his Senate seat. Mail that flooded his Boston office the next week was equally supportive, it was said. A reporter for the *Worcester Evening Gazette*, summing up public reaction to the speech, wrote, "If the Kennedy name has been one of magnetism in national politics, it has been one of magic in Massachusetts."[1]

But newspaper editorials, magazine opinion columns, and television commentary were uniformly and harshly negative nationwide. Any reasoned analysis of the speech found that it had not answered a single question raised by Kennedy's accident report, nor did the speech even attempt to do so. Instead, it had substituted mitigating arguments, claims of heroic efforts at rescue, and appeals for sympathy and political support. That a huge cover-up was being perpetrated on the American people was nearly universally concluded. The media demanded more investigation.

Indicative of the disappointment and disillusionment that even avid Kennedy supporters felt after his television address was the comment of David Halberstam, a Pulitzer Prize-winning journalist and author: "The speech was of such cheapness and bathos as to be a rejection of everything the Kennedys had stood for in candor and style."[2]

Typical of the calls for more investigation, the New York Times editorialized after a few days' reflection, "There are so many gaping holes in the story which he has so assiduously avoided filling, there is such an unmistakable atmosphere of calculated evaluation for the maximum — or, as the case may be, minimum — public effect, that we cannot consider the matter to have been satisfactorily resolved in any sense."[3]

The following day, the Washington Post used even stronger language, writing that Kennedy's unwillingness to be forthright about the Chappaquiddick tragedy was "compelling evidence in support of the ugly suggestion that there was, and still is a careful, cold-blooded conspiracy to cover something up — a suspicion that, as things stand, is easily arrived at."[4]

The Christian Science Monitor in Boston was perhaps the most prophetic about the national implications of the accident and the speech: "It is doubtful if what is often spoken of as the Kennedy aura can ever be won back."[5]

Max Lerner, in his insightful analysis of Ted Kennedy, the person, wrote in 1980, "In its way the speech was a masterpiece of evasions, half-truths, omissions, elisions, shadings of meaning, and appeals to emotion, all contributing to form a mawkish piece of special pleading rather than the bare and honest narrative of events that was called for, and a manful assumption of responsibility."[6]

All of the doubts and demands in the national media brought the focus onto the office of District Attorney Dinis, who had to this point remained as inconspicuous as possible. He had ignored all of Arena's, Steele's, and Mills's requests for help, advice, or involvement in the case, wishing to stay far away from any prosecution of Senator Kennedy. Dinis had continually dismissed the case as simply an automobile accident, appropriately handled by the local authorities. He had been backed in this decision repeatedly by his chief investigator, Lieutenant Killen, who late in life, however, regarded his actions in the case as the biggest stain on his career. But with the public clamor growing, it now appeared that

Dinis's inaction might be worse for his career than involvement in the case.

What Dinis would decide to do was always a question mark. A handsome bachelor of forty-four with dark wavy hair and deep roots in the Portuguese community of New Bedford, he had followed his father, Jacinto, into politics, serving as a city councilman and state senator before being elected Massachusetts district attorney, the youngest ever at thirty-four. Dinis had inherited a rather volatile personality from his father; some would say erratic. While he said his job was simply to see justice done, he was always aware of the political implications of any decision he made. He was up for reelection the next year and would be on the Democratic ticket with Kennedy. Whether or not to become involved was a tough political call for Dinis, one that could be more easily career ending than career boosting.

Dinis's most trusted assistant, Armand Fernandes, also of Portuguese descent, was quick to realize that the D.A.'s office could no longer watch

Edmund S. Dinis, district attorney of the Southern District of Massachusetts, outside the Edgartown Court House at the time of the inquest (© Bettmann/ CORBIS)

the ballgame from the bleachers and needed to pick up a bat and step to the plate. As Fernandes later expressed it, "About twenty seconds after the speech, I knew Eddie [Edmund Dinis] would have to do something."[7]

What would that "something" be? Well, what the case needed was sworn testimony. After all, Arena had never questioned a single attendee of the Lawrence cottage cookout, and he had obtained only short written statements from Kennedy and Crimmins. Grand jury proceedings, where the jury — then rumored to be anxious to get involved — would have the final say about whether there was sufficient evidence to return an indictment against Kennedy, were not at all what Dinis wanted. Further, grand jury proceedings, being secret, would not be the open forum he wanted to showcase his official duties to the public. But an inquest, an investigative hearing into a death to determine whether a crime had been committed, would satisfy Dinis's desires.

An inquest would allow subpoenaing witnesses to give testimony under oath, and the proceedings, at the judge's discretion, could be public (and in the past usually had been). Another advantage of an inquest, in Dinis's thinking, was that while he would be visible in examining witnesses, the proceedings were the responsibility of a judge, who would conduct them and at the end issue a report of his findings. And it would be up to the judge, at its conclusion, to recommend further legal action if he deemed it justified, an off-loading of responsibility that Dinis preferred. Further, the judge's recommendations would not be binding on the district attorney, who would still have a free hand. That seemed made to order to Dinis, so on July 31, six days after Kennedy's Friday-evening speech, Dinis announced he was requesting the assignment of a judge to preside over an inquest.

Inquests, however, had become an outmoded procedure, and few had been held in Massachusetts since train-wreck investigations some eighty years earlier. Thus, the procedure of scheduling an inquest was not clear to Dinis, whose first attempt, directed to the chief justice of the Superior Court, was rebuffed. Instead, he was instructed to file his request with the District Court of Dukes County, Judge Boyle's court. Boyle, who had just sentenced Kennedy for leaving the scene of an accident after causing personal injury, was expected to recuse himself.

After all, he had presided over Kennedy's trial without making any attempt to explore the perplexing circumstances of the accident, agreed with the recommended minimum sentence, and then suspended even that, justifying his decision by stating that Kennedy had already suffered enough. That led to a reasonable expectation of bias if he handled the inquest. However, he did not recuse himself, and that decision was later approved in the appeal — a highly favorable ruling for Kennedy.

Eight days later, Judge Boyle set the date for the inquest as September 3, 1969. Since Massachusetts law gave the judge the power to determine how open the inquest would be, Boyle decided it would be public. However, considering the limited seating capacity of his courtroom (about 120 outside the bar enclosure), he announced that only accredited members of the news media, not the general public, would be admitted to the proceedings. Court Clerk Teller soon posted a list of over 150 media representatives applying for admission.[8]

By requesting an inquest, Dinis was embarking on a delicate balancing act: he said the inquest would not be searching for criminality but was necessary to obtain a complete record of the events surrounding Mary Jo's death. Of course, the reason a complete record was not already known was almost universally attributed to a cover-up, and what was the purpose of a cover-up if there had not been some criminality?

The inquest would allow obtaining statements under oath from the eleven people at the Lawrence cottage party who had never been directly questioned, as well as from Look, Peachey, Richards, and whomever a new investigation by Dinis might turn up. The new investigation, ironically, would be managed by Killen, who had continually and emphatically recommended that Dinis avoid involvement in the politically charged Kennedy case. Killen would be assisted by Bernie Flynn, also a detective lieutenant in the state police. Though they obtained the records of Arena's investigation, he did not participate in the new investigation.

One issue that Dinis wanted resolved definitively was the cause of death as determined by an autopsy. He had had the opportunity to order an autopsy when the body was still on Martha's Vineyard in his jurisdiction, but, wanting at the time to avoid the case, he had tossed the hot potato back to Steele, Mills, and Arena in Edgartown, who failed to request one. After the body was released to the Kopechnes in Pennsylvania, it was no longer under Dinis's jurisdiction. Now, an autopsy would require an exhumation and one in a different state where a favorable court decision would be necessary, not just a prosecutor's order as was sufficient in Massachusetts. Most medical opinions held that embalming would not prevent determining the cause of death.

The recorded cause of death, "asphyxiation by immersion (overturned submerged automobile)," had been determined as much by the circumstance in which the body was found as by Mills's cursory, external examination of the body. Farrar, who had recovered the body, was telling anyone who would listen a different story. He was sure Mary Jo had suffocated when she exhausted the oxygen of the air pocket trapped in the rear-seat footwell of the overturned and submerged car. Certainly, the position and configuration of the body when he recovered it from the wreck strongly indicated this. Further, he saw copious air bubbles come up from the automobile as it was rolled over before being pulled from the water. Farrar had felt that the body was positively buoyant as he moved it out of the car and through the water, a clear indication that there was still a substantial amount of air (or rebreathed carbon dioxide and nitrogen) in the lungs. Typically in a drowning, the lungs become full of water, so the body has no buoyancy and sinks. But the body, Farrar had noted, had not sunk to the bottom of the car in this case. The slightly bloodied froth around the nose and mouth of the corpse could have arisen from suffocation as well as drowning. Farrar publicly maintained that it was likely he would have found Mary Jo still breathing that air pocket had he been notified immediately about the accident. If Farrar's analysis were accepted, Kennedy's nine-hour delay in reporting the accident would take on a far more perilous significance, showing negligence that would support an involuntary manslaughter charge.

Farrar's conclusion was an incendiary addition to the public debate and immediately made him a controversial figure rather than simply a public-safety officer who had done his duty efficiently and made important observations concerning the circumstances of the accident.

Farrar thus became regarded as an advocate instead of a disinterested professional. Unfortunately, this led to his testimony in two court proceedings being sharply curtailed, so that his observations and resultant conjecture, which an autopsy could have perhaps verified or rejected, went largely unexplored and continue to generate controversy.

Judge Boyle held a hearing on August 27 to receive petitions from Kennedy, Gargan, and a group of eight party guests headed by Crimmins concerning their rights at the inquest. Essentially, they asked for the same rights they would have if they were on trial: representation by counsel throughout the proceedings, with counsel's ability to subpoena, examine, and cross-examine witnesses, make motions, and present evidence. In denying the petition the following day, Boyle ruled that such due-process rights had never applied to an inquest in Massachusetts. He did rule that a witness could be represented by counsel during the witness's testimony, and only then, and only to advise the witness on issues of self-incrimination and privileged communication with counsel.

At the hearing, Judge Boyle described what form his findings would take: "I must report in writing when, where, and by what means the person met her death, her name, if known, and all material circumstances attending her death, and name, if known, of any person whose unlawful act or negligence appears to have contributed thereto." His wording was taken almost verbatim from the governing statute. The reference to "negligence" was clearly Kennedy's continuing worry.

Not surprisingly, Kennedy and colleagues were not happy with the inquest procedure Judge Boyle had set, particularly its openness to all the news media and its restrictions on the role of counsel. On September 2, a day before the inquest's scheduled beginning and with all the television and reportorial preparations nearly complete, Kennedy's lawyer, Edward Hanify, obtained an injunction from a justice of the Supreme Judicial Court to halt the inquest until Kennedy and his colleagues' petitions were considered by the full court. Hanify had waited until Justice Paul C. Reardon, known for his strong feelings about pretrial publicity as author of the American Bar Association's code "Free Trial — Free Press," had begun a month-long turn at hearing such petitions.[9] Hanify's argument that the "crescendo of publicity" could "taint" subsequent judicial proceedings met highly receptive ears.[10]

On October 8, argument was held in Boston on the petitions, and the decision was issued on October 30. While noting that Massachusetts law had never required inquests to be secret, the court pointed out that, in recent cases, the U.S. Supreme Court had moved strongly toward protecting defendants from the dangers of pretrial publicity. Thus basing its decision on those federal precedents and its administrative authority over Massachusetts lower courts, the Supreme Judicial Court ruled that "all inquests shall be closed to the public and to all news media" and "the inquest documents shall remain impounded," except for access by the attorney general, the appropriate district attorney, and counsel for anyone "having actual or possible responsibility for the decedent's death." The court stipulated that impoundment would end and public examination would be allowed once the district attorney filed that no prosecution was proposed, an indictment had been sought but not returned, any trial of an inquest-cited person had been completed, or a Superior Court judge had determined that any criminal trial was unlikely.[11]

In these carefully crafted stipulations of impoundment (taking 225 words), the court's omission of any mention of grand-jury access to the inquest record was certainly intentional and thus, it would seem, intentionally obstructionist to any later grand-jury proceedings. After all, should not the record of judicial investigatory proceedings — the inquest — be available to judicial indictment proceedings — the grand jury?

The ruling then laid out principles governing inquests that would later be used to justify preventing grand-jury access to the inquest record: "Inquests are investigatory in character and not accusatory. [Case citations.] They are not part of any criminal proceedings which may ensue. [Case citations.] Under statutes resembling our own, in order to initiate a criminal prosecution, there must be subsequent and independent criminal proceedings. [Case citations.]" The ruling then listed the few highly restricted uses of the inquest record: "It may be that, to show an admission or confession at an inquest or to prove the prior inconsistent statement of a witness, some evidence at an inquest will be admissible at later criminal proceedings in accordance with the usual principles of the law of evidence. The inquest decision itself is not admissible. [Case citations.]"

Apparently this ruling required any grand jury to duplicate the inquest proceedings within a proceedings of its own. This prevention of grand-jury access to the inquest testimony and to Judge Boyle's report would come to haunt the Chappaquiddick accident case.

The ruling did not address a portion of the statute governing inquests in Massachusetts about "witnesses, who may be kept separate so that they cannot converse with each other until they have been examined."[12] That should have been a governing principle enforced by Judge Boyle at the time the inquest date was first set, to prevent the coordination of testimony by witnesses. Instead, we will see, the party guests were not only allowed to speak to each other but were prepared by an attorney for their inquest testimony as a group. While the law just quoted at least strongly recommends that the witnesses be prevented from conversing *before* giving testimony, Boyle, only at the long-delayed beginning of the inquest and after the witnesses had been prepared in a group by an attorney, stated, "Witnesses, *after* testifying, are ordered not to discuss their testimony with anyone except his or her counsel"[13] (emphasis added). Boyle's failure early in the procedure to invoke that part of the inquest law on this issue was certainly a great aid to the Kennedy camp.

While the various proceedings were being held regarding the inquest procedures, Dinis was also filing papers to obtain an exhumation and autopsy. His exhumation petition, cosigned by Medical Examiner Nevin, was sent by certified mail to the Court of Common Pleas of Luzerne County, Pennsylvania. The reason given for an autopsy was to confirm the cause of death by drowning, because an alternate cause would reorient the investigation and the inquest. That seemed to point to featuring Farrar's testimony about asphyxiation being the cause of death. The public interest was also cited, implying the need to put an end to speculation and rumors. To give his petition urgency, Dinis cited one of the purposes of an inquest — to establish whether negligence by someone other than the deceased contributed to causing the death — though such a result was the farthest thing from his goal. To his chagrin, he was informed that Pennsylvania law required the petition to be filed in person. He immediately flew to Wilkes-Barre for a personal filing with Judge Bernard C. Brominski. A hearing was then scheduled for August 25, in time to meet the then-scheduled inquest date of September 3.

Gwen Kopechne had initially favored an autopsy as a way to put to rest the ugly rumors about Mary Jo's behavior and so preserve her daughter's reputation. But Gwen changed her mind and now was adamantly against it. She felt that the drowning conclusion was valid and did not want her daughter's grave disturbed. So prior to the hearing, Joseph Flanagan, representing both Gwen and Joseph Kopechne, filed a motion to dismiss Dinis's petition. Judge Brominski then decided to postpone the hearing and instead rule on the Kopechne motion. Fernandes, arguing the case for Dinis, claimed that scheduling an inquest alone was sufficient reason for allowing an autopsy and so for denying the Kopechne motion. Brominski did not accept that argument and ruled that the Dinis petition did not give sufficiently specific reasons for the autopsy request to be honored. He gave Dinis twenty days to refile his petition.

Dinis did so on September 18, arguing that an autopsy was needed because the slightly bloody froth around the body's nose and mouth could be inconsistent with drowning, again laying the groundwork for exploring Farrar's asphyxiation hypothesis. Brominski decided that this new information required a hearing, which he scheduled for September 29. The Kopechnes then refiled their motion to dismiss the petition. The judge rejected that motion and, with the inquest by that time postponed, set the date of October 20 for testimony on the petition to exhume and autopsy the body.

Dinis and his assistant, Fernandes, presented fourteen witnesses in the two days of testimony, many, such as Arena, the lead-off witness, simply to describe the specifics of the accident. When Fernandes attempted to introduce Kennedy's police accident report, Flanagan's objection to it as hearsay was sustained by Brominski, a really strange ruling. Hearsay is inadmissible because it is "secondhand" knowledge, such as "Sue told me she saw Joe draw the gun," as opposed to "firsthand" knowledge, such as "I saw Joe draw the gun." But Kennedy's police report is an official document giving his firsthand knowledge of the accident and its aftermath. It is not hearsay and should have been admitted. Fernandes, flabbergasted at Brominski's ruling, repeated his efforts to introduce the report until the judge had sustained Flanagan's objections four times. Brominski apparently was content to use stubbornness and authority to cover a stupid ruling.

This episode, of course, raises the question of why Dinis did not call Kennedy himself to testify about the contents of his police report. The best answer may be simply political: with both Kennedy and Dinis up for reelection the following year, Dinis was only trying to do the minimum that his position required.

Dinis's next witness, Farrar, was expected to undermine drowning as the likely cause of death. He wished to present the configuration of the body in the foot well, its buoyancy as he removed it from the wreck, the small amount of water expelled from the body, and the air bubbles seen erupting from the car as it was rolled over as indicating asphyxiation as the likely cause. But when his attorney made an introductory statement to the court, Brominski disallowed almost all of Farrar's expected testimony. Yes, Farrar was a scuba diver, not a physician, and was now being viewed as an advocate, but to prevent his several on-the-scene observations of the body from entering the record seems arbitrary, prejudicial, and simply mistaken. In seeking the truth, an intellectually capable and open-minded person wants to listen to all sides of a question before forming an opinion. Brominski failed this test.

Mills, of course, had to be called to testify. Dinis then had the awkward job of undermining his own witness's finding, but Mills did not budge from his conclusion of drowning and, under cross examination, was unequivocal that there was no evidence of foul play. Mills also testified that Dinis had indicated to him during the week following the tragedy that he had not thought an autopsy was necessary. Dinis then put himself on the stand to rebut this damaging bit of testimony.[14] He claimed he had changed his mind on the need for an autopsy early on the Sunday following the accident but was then told that the body had already been flown to Pennsylvania (which was wrong, because the flight had been delayed). The autopsy hot potato was still being tossed back and forth.

Dinis's next expert was the medical examiner of Philadelphia, Dr. Joseph W. Spellman, whose office handled thousands of autopsies every year. That experience had convinced him that a purely external examination of a body was inadequate. Only an autopsy could reveal internal injuries or conditions that could modify or sometimes even negate a diagnosis based only on an external examination. He did not think the blood-tinged froth was very important but then agreed it could arise from several causes of death, including heart failure, drug overdose, and respiratory depression. That was just the testimony Dinis wanted.

Dr. George G. Katsas, who would likely do the autopsy if it were allowed, testified that an external examination, as done by Mills, was not sufficient to give a definitive cause of death. Katsas also testified that a pathologist experienced in forensic medicine could determine the cause of death in spite of embalming and the passage of several months, important points to Dinis's case.

Dinis called Dr. Cyril H. Wecht to the stand next. With degrees in both medicine and law, he held academic positions at the University of Pittsburgh School of Medicine and Duquesne University School of Law, specializing in forensic sciences. He testified strongly that only an autopsy, not just a ten-minute external examination, was necessary to determine the cause of death definitively. From his experience in autopsying over two dozen exhumed bodies, he believed that an autopsy of Mary Jo's body would produce a conclusive answer. With that, Dinis rested his case.

The Kopechnes' attorney, Flanagan, then called the deputy chief medical examiner of Maryland, Dr. Werner Spitz, who testified that it would be next to impossible to distinguish between death from drowning and death from asphyxiation after burial. However, while Farrar had been cut off from giving his asphyxiation evidence and hypothesis, Dr. Spitz was inadvertently — and to Flanagan's chagrin — allowed to testify that the blood-tinged froth observed by Mills was evidence of struggled breathing of air before death, thus suggesting that asphyxiation could have been the cause. "She breathed, that girl. She wasn't dead instantaneously," Spitz testified.[15] This dramatic turn of events in favor of Dinis, however, was somewhat nullified when Spitz's boss, Chief Medical Examiner Dr. Henry Freimuth, testified that the blood-tinged froth was also typical of drowning.

Near the end of testimony, Brominski made a curious ruling, inconsistent with his disallowance of Kennedy's police accident report, when he allowed Kennedy's television speech into the record. But without the former, Dinis could not exploit the differences between the two. It is not clear, however, that those differences have any relevance to the cause of death issue.

While both Judge Brominski's exhumation decision and the Supreme Judicial Court's decision on Kennedy's petition were being awaited, an event hastened by the Chappaquiddick tragedy occurred in Edgartown Harbor. This was the launching on Sunday, October 26, of a new three-car, two-ended ferry, *On Time II*, to replace the overworked old two-car, one-ended ferry. Ferry owner Jared Grant had built it himself in his Katama backyard. It was needed for the "clamoring reporters and jammering gawkers," in *Vineyard Gazette* parlance.[16] Tourists were lining up in their cars for blocks to take the ferry to see Dike Bridge and get a photo of themselves in front of it. Many came for a souvenir of a splinter of the bridge's wood or a scoop of nearby sand, which enterprising youngsters were happy to sell them. Chappaquiddick's few residents grumbled that the stream of traffic was spoiling "our Chappy."

On December 8, Judge Brominski, considering the testimony as a whole, ruled that evidence of a cause of death other than drowning was unpersuasive, and so he was willing to consider the Kopechnes' strong objection. He ruled against an exhumation and autopsy. When Dinis decided not to appeal the decision, the way was then cleared for Judge Boyle to schedule the inquest. He set the date as January 5, 1970.

Chapter 8

The Inquest

The shadiest event in the lead-up to the inquest was related by Leo Damore in his book, *Senatorial Privilege*, from long interviews with Bernie Flynn, the state police detective assisting Killen in the D.A.'s investigation. Flynn described in detail how he, acting on his own, met surreptitiously at the Washington, D.C., airport with a lawyer, Herbert J. Miller, Jr., representing Kennedy. The meeting had been arranged secretly through Stephen Smith, Kennedy's brother-in-law, with the purpose of revealing all witnesses and evidence that Dinis would present at the inquest. Flynn explained, "My main purpose is, I don't want Ted Kennedy to get caught in a big lie that could really make him go down the drain. The reason I'm there is not to have Ted Kennedy go into the inquest and start lying again. Because in my opinion he'd already lied in the police report and the TV speech, and I liked the guy. I knew he had presidential ambitions."[1] The surreptitious manner used to arrange and carry out the meeting speaks loudly that it was at least highly improper and insubordinate and perhaps illegal.

In late December, as the inquest date neared, Flynn again contacted Smith to tell him that no new information of importance had been discovered in the D.A.'s investigation, so Kennedy need not worry about anything unexpected being sprung on him during the inquest. The message was clear: Kennedy can stick to his new story, and there will be no problem. Flynn minced no words in his interview with Damore: "This time when he tells his lie in the inquest, he can stick with the lie, and they have to swallow it."[2]

Knowing which witnesses would testify and what information they would present was invaluable information for Kennedy's testimony — or defense, as it may be called, even though an inquest is just investigatory, not accusatory. His lawyers, like the lawyers for his fellow partygoers, then knew what to prepare the testimony for or against: which subjects to avoid and which to mention, which words to use and which to steer clear of.

Since he obviously needed consistent testimony from the cottage cookout crowd, Kennedy furnished a pair of lawyers to represent the five young women and three of the men at the party (at a cost of nearly $32,000).[3] Gargan and Markham, more intimately connected with the events, chose to be represented by their own counsel, Joseph P. Donahue, and Kennedy, of course, had a battery of attorneys, including Edward B. Hanify and Robert G. Clark, Jr. It is important to note that Paul J. Redmond and Daniel Daley, Sr., whom Kennedy hired to represent the cookout group,[4] prepared the eight together for their inquest testimony. No wonder they all gave such consistent testimony! As columnist James B. Stewart wrote in the New York Times concerning another scandal, "A little-discussed but open secret among defense lawyers and prosecutors alike is that who pays the legal fees often decides the outcome of an investigation."[5] Stewart also quoted John C. Coffee, Jr., Berle Professor of Law at Columbia University, as saying, "'Lawyers know very well how to coach witnesses on what to say without telling them to lie.'"[6] Both of these insights are highly relevant to the testimony at the Kopechne inquest.

The interesting question, of course, is why did any of the cookout guests need a lawyer? What was it they saw, heard, or experienced that they — or more likely Kennedy — did not want openly, fully, and honestly related at the inquest? You can surmise from what has been presented here that one of the hidden facts was the true identity of the front-seat passenger when Kennedy drove off the bridge. This passenger would know of Kennedy's condition and actions before, during, and immediately afterward. Others may have known who that person was and had partial knowledge of the accident.

So how should one approach the inquest testimony? In a country that prides itself on its rule of law, there is a natural inclination to trust testimony given under oath. But that would certainly be naive here. Before the inquest began, there was an almost universal belief, fueled by gaps, unexplained actions, and unlikely explanations in Kennedy's police report and television address, that a cover-up was occurring. This belief was compounded by his refusal to submit to questioning by the press corps. Self-protective testimony, including lying, can be expected from anyone in danger of indictment, as Kennedy was. Thus, a healthy dose of skepticism should accompany a reading of the inquest transcript. As expressed earlier, disinterested people's testimony should be preferred over interested parties' testimony when conflicts occur, nuances differ, or protective testimony seems likely.

The entire cookout crowd were loyal Kennedy supporters. Open and full testimony from them cannot be expected. In evaluating each answer to a question, one must ask: is there a reason why the witness would not give a complete and truthful answer, wishing instead to protect Kennedy or possibly the witness? It was a small, close-knit group in the cottage that night, and it was an isolated incident, making contradictions in testimony more easily avoidable. And it was easy to claim memory loss to obscure a situation. Tannenbaum would even testify she could not remember being told how Mary Jo died!

There is an even more troublesome reason to be skeptical of some aspects of the inquest: the improper pressures secretly brought to bear on Judge Boyle. Farrar has revealed to the author for the first time some shocking news. Dorothy Commins, who was Boyle's secretary throughout the Chappaquiddick investigation and inquest, later worked for Farrar at the Turf 'N Tackle shop. She told him in confidence, as best he remembers her words, "You can't imagine the intensity of communications and directions coming down from Boston to Judge Boyle to control the whole procedure."[7] Whether those communications originated from judicial or political sources was left unsaid, but either would have been at least improper. Perhaps the most revealing word Commins used was "intensity," for it implies repeated calls, which would occur only if "Boston" were receiving new information regularly about the inquest progress and testimony. Since the inquest was closed-door, some participant must have been keeping the powers in "Boston" informed. Farrar, in relating this to the author, said he felt free to convey this confidence now that Commins was deceased. It is a disturbing revelation. It goes a long way toward understanding Boyle's Kennedy-protecting behavior at several points during the inquest and, after being persuaded of Kennedy's negligence in Kopechne's death, his abdication of responsibility at its conclusion.

Despite the cookout crowd's carefully choreographed testimony at the inquest, *we find that Tretter's testimony unlocks the remaining mysteries and confirms the identity of Kennedy's front-seat companion on that fateful drive to Dike Bridge.* Tretter's testimony, surprisingly, was not appreciated and so not explored during the inquest. Still more surprisingly, it has not been understood by any analyst in the several decades since the accident! Only Sherrill puzzled over it but, baffled about its implications, formed no conclusions.[8] It isn't, however, that obscure.

The *Inquest re: Mary Jo Kopechne* was opened by Judge Boyle at 9:00 A.M., January 5, 1970, in the red-brick District Courthouse of Dukes County on Main Street in Edgartown. His opening statement gave the proceedings' purpose: "The primary object of an inquest is to ascertain the facts to decide the question of whether or not criminal proceedings shall be instituted against the person or persons responsible for the death."[9] As will be seen below, there were continual errors of omission in ascertaining the facts, but in the end, the most egregious error was Boyle's refusal to follow this stated purpose based on his own official findings of fact.

James A. Boyle, judge of the Dukes County District Court, who presided over the Kopechne inquest (© Bettmann/CORBIS)

The proceedings were held in secret, but a horde of reporters

Surviving boiler-room girls, from left to right, Rosemary Keough, Maryellen Lyons, Nance Lyons, Susan Tannenbaum, and Esther Newburgh, at the airport following their inquest testimony (© Bettmann/CORBIS)

waited outside, in the nippy, damp weather of a Vineyard January day with a few inches of snow on the ground, for any scrap of news for their curious national readership. But few witnesses said anything as they emerged into the elbowing and questioning mob. Press facilities — telephones, desks, etc. — had been set up across the side street in the basement of the Old Whaling Church, a glistening white landmark with six mammoth Doric columns fronting on Main Street. But the facilities' usefulness was modest, as news was scarce.

Kennedy, accompanied by both his lead attorney, Edward B. Hanify, and by Robert G. Clark, Jr., was called as the first witness.[10] Kennedy stuck to his new story, just as Detective Flynn had surreptitiously advised him to do. Kennedy testified that he left the cottage at 11:15 P.M. with Mary Jo sitting in the front seat and with no one else in the car. He said they were intending to return to their hotel rooms in Edgartown and Katama. In glaring omissions that presaged much of what was to come, he was not asked why he, as host, was walking out on his own party, why he did not offer others a ride back to their booked accommodations, or why he did not even say goodnight to his guests.

Early in his testimony, Kennedy denied emphatically that he had ever been on Chappaquiddick before the fateful weekend. But in 1980, after a two-and-a-half-month investigation, the *New York Post* published an exposé of Kennedy's regatta weekend parties of 1966 and 1967 (the latter began a two-year affair with a named countess), finding several people who would swear they had seen, knew of, or been with Kennedy on Chappaquiddick before 1969.[11]

In contradiction to Look's reliable observations, Kennedy testified he passed no other car, he saw no one on the road between the cottage and Dike Bridge, he did not stop along the way, he did not drive onto Cemetery Road, and he did not back up his car at any time. Curiously, he was not then asked why he turned onto Dike Road or why, after realizing he was off the paved road and on a sand and gravel road, he did not turn around. Since that was an issue on which Kennedy had changed his story from his police report to his television speech — in fact, he ignored the issue altogether in the latter — it was certainly a subject worth questioning.

While denying all aspects of Look's observations, Kennedy unwittingly gave information supporting Look's time of the accident as 12:45 A.M., not an hour and a half earlier. Kennedy testified that after exiting the submerged car, he "was swept away by the tide that was flowing at an extraordinary rate" southward, thirty or forty feet toward the closed end of Poucha Pond, before he managed to reach the east shore.[12] Thus, according to Kennedy, the accident occurred during a strong incoming tide and thus well after low tide. Low tide is known to have occurred at that location the following morning at 11:30, the only time the wrecker could remove the Olds 88 from the pond. Thus, low tide occurred there also at close to 11:30 the previous evening, meaning that there was slack water when Kennedy claimed the accident occurred. On the other hand, at 12:45 A.M. there was an incoming tide that would have swept Kennedy southward, as he testified. In short, Kennedy's own testimony inadvertently supported Look's chronology. Dinis did not grasp, or wished to ignore, the contradiction between the tidal phase and Kennedy's claimed timing and so had no testimony about the tides introduced. This was a serious oversight, particularly for someone living near salt water and thus conscious of the ocean's rhythms.

Kennedy held to his story of repeatedly diving to rescue Mary Jo, but there were no probing questions to elucidate those efforts, which could have made them more believable or, more likely, less believable. He testified that just before he undertook his rescue attempts, the submerged headlights were still on, so why not ask how long they remained on? He said he stayed at the wreck site for thirty to forty minutes. Since it could be determined how long the headlights could remain on in salt water until the battery was drained, his answer could have either supported or undermined his credibility. A natural question would have been: while the headlights were still on, did he look in either the side or back windows? Again, Dinis did not seem to be probing.

Kennedy denied seeing any house with a light lit as he walked back to the Lawrence cottage. He testified how dark the night was and how difficult it was to walk along Dike Road, which was correct because the moon had set at 10:26 P.M. With no city-lights glow in the sky on rural Chappaquiddick, the night was truly black. Thus the backdoor light at Dyke House and the children's bedroom light at the Smith cottage across Dike Road should have been particularly eye-catching. Astoundingly, after this denial, he was not asked why he, supposedly frantically wanting to save Mary Jo minutes before, did not then stop and pound on the door of *any* cottage — darkened or lit — in hopes of getting help! Of course, if he did not know that Mary Jo was in the car, as presented here, his behavior was understandable. But he had to stick to his new story, and he was allowed to do so unchallenged.

Another bit of Kennedy's testimony undermines his credibility and his timing of events. He estimated he had spent fifteen to twenty minutes attempting to rescue Mary Jo, fifteen to twenty minutes resting on the bank from his exertion, and fifteen minutes walking to the cottage before enlisting Gargan and Markham to return to the bridge for another rescue attempt. Asked what time it was when Kennedy arrived back at Dike Bridge, he said he had seen the clock in the Valiant and gave the time as being 12:20 A.M., consistent with these time intervals and time of the accident that he had previously claimed. However, research by the *Boston Globe* Spotlight Team five years after the accident found that the particular Valiant driven that weekend had no clock, either factory or owner installed[13] — one more bit of fabricated testimony.

In answer to a question as to who had access to his Olds 88 that evening, Kennedy replied in part and rather uncertainly, "I believe Mr. Tretter borrowed the car to return to Edgartown briefly. I couldn't say of my own knowledge that he used that car rather than the Valiant, but he may very well have."[14] Dinis then dropped the subject, in spite of its relevance to finding Keough's handbag in the submerged Oldsmobile 88. It was one more failure to pursue a needed line of questioning.

Kennedy's confusion on a few topics is hard to explain. Since he had shown no confusion in the hours and days after the accident, it is unlikely to be attributable to reappearing psychological trauma six months later. Nervousness from the tension of telling a largely untrue story is probably the best answer.

The issue of whether the driver's-seat window was open is an example of this. In his questioning, he first said, "Some of the windows were open and some were closed." When asked about the driver's-seat window, he replied, "I would expect it was open." Then when asked if he remembered that, he said, "I don't remember that." Immediately after stating, "I really have no personal knowledge as to which windows were open or closed," he was asked whether the driver's-seat window was open, and he replied, "Yes, it was." A few questions later, he described groping for the window under water and testified, "The window was closed." Then in answer to a further question about those moments under water, he replied, "The [driver's-seat] window was open."[15]

The driver's-seat window was found open in the submerged wreck and its door locked. Thus, the window was certainly Kennedy's escape route and hence, one would think, memorable. Curiously, he testified that he remembered groping for the window and door handle in some detail but claimed he could not remember how he exited the vehicle. From his accident investigation experience, crash expert Robert Dubois has found this most unusual.[16] Further scrambling this issue, Kennedy apparently remembered and described his exit from the car to his personal physician soon after arriving in Hyannis Port later in the day of the accident, because Dr. Robert D. Watt, in his affidavit filed at the inquest, wrote, "at the last moment he grabbed the side of an open window and pulled himself out."[17] This bit of filed testimony, most certainly based on Kennedy's statements to him, has gone unnoticed by many writers on the Chappaquiddick tragedy.

Another interesting contradiction in Kennedy's testimony that went unexplored is his characterization of the underwater visibility while he was still in the car. He described it as "pitch black," "the blackness" (twice), and "complete blackness."[18] This seems to be more of an over-dramatization than a true observation, because he also testified that "the headlights of the car were still on" well after he had escaped the car and was on dry land. The headlights, later found to have been on high or bright beam, would have produced a substantial glow, helping Kennedy to orient himself in the overturned, submerged automobile and to exit. Perhaps he had his eyes closed and didn't remember that. The light should have also helped his front-passenger-seat companion to scramble out of the car. However, Mary Jo, uninjured but groggy, confused, and unobserved, did not find an escape route from the overturned, rear-seat compartment where her body was found.

Kennedy, aware that evidence of drunkenness at the time of the accident could possibly lead to a charge of involuntary manslaughter, testified he was "absolutely sober."[19] He stated that he had had only a third of a bottle of beer at the Shiretown Inn and two rum-and-Cokes at the Chappaquiddick party before a ten-o'clock dinner. He estimated that each drink had two ounces of rum. Under questioning, he failed to mention the three rum-and-Cokes that he tossed down in twenty minutes after the Friday race, aboard the winning *Bettawin* with Stan Moore.[20] At the end of testimony, realizing he had not mentioned these drinks and with testimony by Moore expected, Kennedy received permission to offer a further statement: "There was some modest intake of alcohol . . . after the race."[21] Once again, Dinis did not ask for a more detailed answer. As it turned out, Moore was not called to testify, so this vague statement was allowed to stand. If Kennedy was speaking truthfully that three two-ounce liquor drinks in twenty minutes was "modest intake" for him, one can only wonder at what his heavy drinking was like.

His testimony of having just two drinks at the party is certainly difficult to believe. Killen's investigation revealed that Crimmins had purchased the liquor for the party in South Boston. In testimony, Crimmins stated he had bought three half-gallons of vodka, four fifths of scotch, two bottles of rum, and two cases of beer for the Chappaquiddick shindig. Apparently well over two drinks per person were expected. Forensic evidence indicated Mary Jo had had three or four drinks (or more, depending on just when she left the party), and it is hard to believe that Kennedy was out-drunk by a petite female guest.

After reading the transcript of Kennedy's several hours of questioning, one cannot help feeling a great disappointment in the supposed investigatory function of the inquest. The questioning by Dinis and Judge Boyle was perfunctory not probing, passive not analytically active, spontaneous not well planned. Vague and unspecific answers to questions were allowed to stand, while in answer to some questions, Kennedy was permitted to launch into his obviously rehearsed story time and again.

An example of the latter situation occurred when he was asked what had prevented him from seeking assistance for a rescue beyond the help of Gargan and Markham. Rather than being forced to answer the question, Kennedy was allowed to launch into a long soliloquy of irrelevant thoughts, to carry his version of events forward to the time he was at the Shiretown Inn. Then, without having obtained an answer to his original question, Dinis passively resumed his questioning about that later time, omitting questions about all the poorly described intervening activities. The inquest's most glaring omission was a failure to ask Kennedy why he fled to Edgartown.

Another glaring example of the inadequacy of the questioning concerns where Mary Jo was in the car. Early in his testimony, Kennedy stated she was in the front passenger seat, but in the long soliloquy just mentioned, he said, "even though I knew that Mary Jo was dead, and believe[d] firmly that she was in the *back of the car . . .* "[22] (emphasis added). This contradiction in Kennedy's testimony went completely unquestioned and unexamined, illustrating just how little Dinis or Judge Boyle wished to ensnare Kennedy or to open up anything new. That statement still invites curiosity.

Allowed to continue his soliloquy, Kennedy described his swim across the channel to Edgartown. Though minutes before Kennedy said that he had been too "exhausted" to help in the supposed second rescue attempt, he now simply "dove in the water" to undertake a difficult and dangerous swim across the darkened, tide-swept channel.[23] He testified, "The tide began to draw me out . . . and I remembered being swept down toward the direction of the Edgartown Light [northeastward] and well out into the darkness."[24] Thus, Kennedy claimed he swam in an *outflowing* tide. But both Kennedy's and Look's timing of events puts Kennedy swimming the channel (if true) at about 1:30 A.M., and at that time there was a strong *incoming* tide that would have swept him toward the inner harbor, southwestward, not northeastward toward Edgartown Light and the beach he said he landed on. Low tide had occurred at Edgartown at 9:54 P.M.[25] Huck Look, crossing the channel on the Edgartown Yacht Club's launch at 12:35 A.M., observed that the tide "was running *in* strongly"[26] (emphasis added). Thus, Kennedy's vivid description of his swim does not match reality, loses its credibility, and, for a second time, inadvertently supports Look's timing of events. Probably the only true aspect of his swimming-the-channel story is his surreptitious landing on the dark, relatively secluded beach of the Edgartown Light, probably in a dinghy.

When Dinis tried to explore Kennedy's lack of reporting the accident in a timely way, he was cut off by Judge Boyle, who, with Kennedy removed from the courtroom, explained he was uninterested in the aftermath of the accident, only whether there had been criminal negligence in causing Mary Jo's death.[27] But if the "aftermath" began at Mary Jo's death, when would negligence have occurred?

By Farrar's hypothesis, based on his several observations, that Mary Jo lived by breathing the pocket of air for some time, perhaps even an hour, the "aftermath" did not start until after Kennedy had failed to knock on the Malm or Smith cottages' doors, to ring the alarm at the volunteer fire station, or to call the police from the ferry-shed telephone. By that interpretation — certainly one worth exploring at an inquest — Kennedy's failure to take any of those actions constituted negligence under Massachusetts law and so would open up the possibility of an involuntary manslaughter charge.

Dinis likely did not want to pursue that particular line of questioning. The consequences were too dire for his own career, let alone Kennedy's fate. But Dinis must have felt that he should be allowed to delve into the aftermath of the accident in hopes of answering the public's many questions. In the off-the-record discussion, Judge Boyle partially relented and permitted Dinis to explore some of the aftermath. But Dinis, after asking Kennedy why he had not sought assistance immediately, lapsed into passive mode, allowing Kennedy to launch into his rehearsed and unsatisfying story.

Judge Boyle did allow Kennedy's police accident report and television speech to be admitted as exhibits in the proceedings, but he did not allow Dinis to explore either of them in detail or the several important differences between them. That suggests that Boyle was protecting Kennedy.

So Kennedy's testimony concluded with him able to "stick with the lie," as Flynn had advised him to do, and had revealed little that was new, except for the tidal observations that undermined his own timing of events.

Additional Testimony

The district attorney's interest in understanding Kennedy's nine-hour delay in reporting the accident is evident in his calling a New England Telephone and Telegraph representative, A. Robert Malloy, as the second witness. At the inquest, his testimony proved to be of no value, but ten years later, a *New York Times* investigation revealed that the company had not introduced as evidence three of the four lists of relevant telephone calls charged to various credit cards used by Kennedy and brought to the inquest.[28] The subpoena had requested "records of all calls made with credit card or cards of Edward M. Kennedy on July

18 and 19 of 1969, location of number called and the identity of party to whom number is listed, time of day when call was made," which is both broad in scope and specific in requested detail. A careful reading of the testimony indicates that the withholding of the three lists — contrary to the subpoena — resulted from a combination of artful wording by the witness's attorney, who was allowed to insert himself in the witness's testimony against the announced inquest rules, and obtuse questioning almost entirely by Judge Boyle, who simply didn't understand telephone credit cards.

By bringing records of "all calls" to the inquest as required, New England Tel showed it understood the breadth of the subpoena, but its inquest attorney, Charles R. Parrott, claimed during the *New York Times* investigation that "the subpoena only reached the New England Telephone company." That contradicts Malloy's statement at the inquest prior to Parrott's interruption: "I was able to investigate three of his accounts, one in Boston, one in Washington, and one in Virginia." Parrott went on to say that it was not his "place to volunteer, or Mr. Malloy's place to volunteer, anything except in response to questions"; that is, it was not his or Malloy's duty to produce "records of all calls" requested by the subpoena, a hard position to defend legally. In fact, it was Parrott's interference that prevented Malloy from answering Dinis's question, "Will you produce the records that show those specific calls emanating from Edgartown or Chappaquiddick for those particular dates, July 18th and 19th?"[29] Before Malloy could answer, Parrott interrupted to say, in part, "To assist the Court, he has made a compilation of those which I think would be helpful." The list then handed to Dinis contained only those calls made on Kennedy's personal credit card. Parrott's maneuver diverted the Court's attention to a list of calls on this one account, on which the recorded calls were made entirely by others, such as Gargan.

Parrott's injection of himself into Malloy's testimony, in fact, was a direct violation of Judge Boyle's rules for accompanying attorneys' participation. But Boyle, totally confused about credit-card accounts, failed to disallow Parrott's remarks and return testimony to Dinis's question.

Kennedy's own calls that day were made on a New York Telephone credit card charged to the Park Agency, a New York company that administers Kennedy family trusts and financial affairs. A record of those calls was on one of the withheld lists. Those records no longer existed at the time of the *New York Times* investigation. In response to that investigation, Kennedy said that all the calls he referred to in his inquest testimony were made on the New York Tel card. In spite of Dinis's interest in calling Malloy as his second witness, he (and Judge Boyle also) never realized that the calls Kennedy admitted to were not a part of the one list entered into the inquest record. So he never reopened testimony on credit-card calls, and Kennedy's full telephone record was never entered in the testimony — one more example of Dinis's (and Boyle's) unanalytical thinking and questioning.

Why did New England Tel behave in this manner? Kenneth Kappel, who wrote *Chappaquiddick Revealed,* believes he knows.[30] He found that Kennedy's lead attorney, Hanify, was a director of New England Tel at the time and so may have influenced the legal strategy for handling the telephone records.

Further, John J. O'Connor, the manager of the company's Falmouth, Massachusetts, office on which the subpoena was served, told investigators that executives at the Boston headquarters had considered telephone use in the Chappaquiddick tragedy in the first days after the accident and he had been directed to investigate just three or four days after the accident — illegally because it was not authorized yet by a subpoena — any presence of a telephone at the Lawrence cottage (it was locked away from the guests) and possible calls made by Kennedy from the Shiretown Inn. O'Connor was scheduled to testify at the inquest until the last moment, when he was replaced by Malloy, perhaps to keep those early illegal phone-company investigations private.

Could the unrevealed phone-call lists, if introduced at the inquest, have changed the course of the investigation? Not knowing what they were, of course, prevents any firm answer, but Parrott's successful maneuver to avoid their introduction suggests that there was something to hide. But what? The conversations themselves were not recorded, so only the parties and times called would have been revealed. And they may just have been family members and the coterie of advisors that later gathered in Hyannis Port to write Kennedy's television speech, not great revelations. Further, the present account shows that there was no reason for Kennedy to make phone calls before he learned of Mary Jo's death the following morning, and his calls after that are known.

The next partygoer to testify was LaRosa, probably because it was he whom Kennedy had asked to get Gargan and Markham when Kennedy returned to the cottage from the accident. LaRosa testified he had not seen Kennedy or Kopechne leave the party. LaRosa described taking two walks after midnight, the first one with the Lyons sisters and Tannenbaum heading away from the ferry toward Wasque Point and back. The second one, surprisingly, offered substantial support for Look's timing of events and was contrary to Kennedy's — but with a minor inconsistency. This second walk was taken only with the Lyons sisters, at about 12:45 A.M., toward the ferry. They saw a car slow down as it passed them going in the direction of the ferry. A short time later, a car approached them coming from the ferry direction and stopped, and the driver asked whether he could be of help. One of the girls said something like, "Shove off," for which LaRosa, the soberest of the partygoers, apologized and said they were staying nearby.[31]

Look's later testimony described this encounter along the road as occurring shortly after his encounter with the Kennedy car at the Dike Road intersection (apparently the car that passed the walkers shortly before). In his inquest testimony, Look recalled two women and a man walking in a line (along the centerline of the road, according to LaRosa) and that the women "were very jovial, happy" and "very happy-go-lucky,"[32] but in an earlier interview Look described them as "doing some kind of dance in the road, a hootchy-kootchy or a conga,"[33] an incidental observation that attests to the partygoers' level of gaiety at that post-midnight hour. He recalled the taller woman, apparently Nance Lyons, saying, "Shove off, buddy," when he offered them a lift.[34] The man — LaRosa — said they were staying at a nearby cottage that he pointed in the direction of. This encounter gives further corroborative evidence for Look's timing of the accident. However, LaRosa said that the threesome's walk occurred after Gargan and Markham had left the cottage in the Valiant, which does not fit with any testified timing and, after much head scratching, seems most likely to be just a mixed-up memory. In another abject failure in questioning, no one asked LaRosa whether he recognized the passing car as Kennedy's, whether he noticed the number of its occupants, or even whether Kennedy was still at the cottage when they left.

Tretter was called next to the stand, with his testimony carrying over into the second day of the inquest. He testified that he had not seen either Kennedy or Mary Jo leave the party. Also, he had heard no conversation that would indicate that either of them was about to leave: no "Goodnight," "I'm bailing out," or "I want to catch the last ferry," the sort of remarks that would be expected if either were actually turning in for the night.

Tretter offered testimony that he, accompanied by Keough, left the Lawrence cottage between 9:00 and 9:30 P.M. in Kennedy's Olds 88 to return to Edgartown to borrow a radio from the Shiretown Inn for the party.[35] It was on this trip, Keough contended in later testimony, that she left her purse in the car, thus supposedly accounting for its presence in the submerged wreck after the accident.

Tretter's testimony of using the Kennedy car is confusing. Before testifying about this later trip, Tretter was questioned about an errand he ran back to Edgartown at about eight o'clock that evening to buy ice, tonic, and cigarettes for the party:[36]

> District Attorney Dinis: Would you tell us what car you were using at this time?
>
> Tretter: I am not — there were three of them and I am not sure which of the three I used at that time.
>
> Dinis: You say there were three cars at the party; Mr. Kennedy's car, the rented car, and Mr. LaRosa's car. Are these the three cars you are talking about?
>
> Tretter: Yes, I had occasion to drive three separate cars all intermixed. [This is the only testimony of a third car at the party. He later recanted, saying there were only two cars at the party.]

Shortly after this testimony, Tretter was questioned about his second errand to obtain a radio for the party:[37]

> Dinis: Tell us which car you used.

Tretter: The Senator's.
Dinis: Tell us from whom you got the keys.
Tretter: Mr. Crimmins.
Dinis: Do you remember asking him for the keys?
Tretter: I believe I did, because he would normally have them.

So from confusion about which car he used for the first errand and even the number of cars available, he offered a firm memory of the car he used for the second errand, until his answer was explored, and then descended into uncertainty and supposition. Neighbor Dodie Silva's report, described earlier, of recognizing Kennedy's car and the same driver for both errands removes the uncertainties here.

Then, in highly significant testimony that surprisingly has never before been adequately analyzed, Tretter related that he took a forty or so minute walk toward the ferry along Chappaquiddick Road, almost to the intersection with Dike Road, and then returned along the same route. His walk began soon after the time that he noticed that Kennedy and Mary Jo were not there. The testimony was as follows:[38]

Dinis: Now, what were the activities at the party after they left or after you became aware that Mr. Kennedy and Miss Kopechne were not there?
Tretter: I left the cottage for a walk.
Dinis: With whom?
Tretter: Miss Keough.

The ambiguity in this abbreviated question and answer is important. Did he agree that he *left* with Keough or that he simply *had a walk* with her? In other words, did he begin the walk with her or alone? He had just used the first-person singular in saying, "I left the cottage for a walk," not "We left . . ." or "I left with . . ." This was not a careless usage, because in his three other direct inquest statements about *beginning* the walk, he used the first-person singular each time. His other descriptions of beginning the walk at that point of the questioning were "I left 11:30 or quarter of 12:00 . . ."[39] and "I walked out of the cottage. . . ."[40] When the questioning later returned to the walk, his description was more detailed but still indicated strongly that he began the walk alone: "I became aware that they [Kennedy and Mary Jo] were not there when *I went out for a walk* and had to go by where the two cars were parked and there was only one car, the white Valiant, and I did not see either Senator Kennedy or Miss Kopechne."[41] Note that in all four of his statements about beginning the walk, Tretter did not add "with Miss Keough" or "and was accompanied by Miss Keough," and neither did he use the first-person plural "we." Any of these would have been normal wording if he had begun the walk with her. *The record thus strongly supports the conclusion that Tretter began the walk alone.* Also important in Tretter's last statement quoted is the presence of the Valiant at the cottage when he left, which shows that both Gargan and Markham were still there and that Kennedy had not yet arrived back there.

The estimated departure time and duration for this walk are far less important than its occurrence relative to Tretter's observations of the Valiant just mentioned. For the record, the uncertain times offered are the following: Tretter testified the walk occurred between about 11:30 P.M. (or 11:45 P.M.) and 12:15 A.M. Keough, however, later testified the walk began between 11:40 and 11:55 P.M. and lasted forty-five minutes to an hour, but then, after several more questions, she interrupted Dinis to correct herself, saying that the walk had begun between 12:15 and 12:30 A.M. (which is discussed below). The main importance of the timing of the walk is that it occurred after the departure of Kennedy, his front-seat companion, and Mary Jo in Kennedy's car and before the departure of the Valiant carrying Gargan, Markham, and Kennedy following the accident.

Tretter's Unrecognized Revelation

During this walk, Tretter testified, he saw the Valiant drive past, heading away from the cottage: "When we went on the first walk it was necessary to step off the road a few times for automobiles, and one of the cars I thought I recognized was the white Valiant."[42] (Note for later discussion the important use of "we" at this point of the walk, the passage of the Valiant.) He confirmed this testimony of the Valiant passing in later questioning by Judge Boyle. Since Kennedy, Gargan, and Markham were in the Valiant when it passed, we can conclude with certainty that Kennedy had arrived back at the cottage following his accident during the early part of Tretter's walk. But Tretter's walk covered the stretch of Chappaquiddick Road that Kennedy had to walk in returning from the accident!

Thus Tretter had to encounter Kennedy and his front-seat companion, both of whom were dripping wet and shaken but with no serious injuries, walking back to the cottage from the accident.

The inability of Dinis, Fernandes, and Judge Boyle to deduce this from the testimony and then to pursue it is certainly their greatest failure in questioning during the entire inquest. Even more surprising, given the long time for analysis, is that no author writing about the Chappaquiddick tragedy has reached this very important — and, it would seem, straightforward — conclusion either! The only mention of this testimony in previous books, as noted earlier, was by Sherrill, who, being puzzled by it, ended simply by saying there had been a great deal of lying or forgetfulness in the testimony.[43] A close reading of Tretter's testimony about the walk does not support that; it seems direct and forthcoming. What was lacking at the inquest and all the time since is logical thinking.

Accepting that Tretter began his walk alone, that he had to encounter Kennedy and his front-seat companion walking on Chappaquiddick Road, and that both Tretter and Keough testified that they returned from the walk to the cottage together, one is driven to infer that Keough joined Tretter on his walk at that encounter. *This firm — and new! — deduction from testimony thus shows that Kennedy had a surviving front-seat companion and points strongly to her identity being Rosemary Keough.*

Under the circumstances, it is understandable that Kennedy would wish to avoid involvement with his front-seat companion. So this fortuitous encounter would have allowed her to turn around, proceed on an extended walk with Tretter, dry off and collect herself from the ordeal, and establish an activity that could be corroborated if needed. Kennedy, intent on establishing his own alibi for what he then thought was a simple auto accident, continued on to the cottage, spoke to

LaRosa, and was accompanied by Gargan and Markham in the Valiant back past Tretter and Keough, as they walked together. Tretter then used "we" in describing the Valiant passing — his first use of "we" in place of "I" in describing the walk, as noted above. Importantly, this explains why Kennedy's surviving front-seat companion — Keough — did not arrive back at the cottage with Kennedy following the accident. The absence of any such observation has misled other analysts of the tragedy from considering a second survivor.

Both Tretter and Keough testified that, upon returning to the cottage, they found it empty, except for Crimmins in bed, and both cars gone. Tretter testified that he assumed "that we had missed the return of people who had gone back [to Edgartown in the Valiant]."[44] Notice again at this point of the walk that Tretter used "we," as he also did in three more statements about the walk, confirming a consistent and meaningful switch from "I" to "we." His testimony of an empty cottage, one might think, would trigger questioning about possible encounters with some of the cookout crowd on that walk, but it didn't. Even an offer of new information was ignored: in answer to a question by Judge Boyle, Tretter offered to clarify where everyone was, saying in part, "I found out the next morning where people had gone by inquiry, but at that time I didn't."[45] This is, perhaps, the clearest example of Boyle and Dinis not wishing to open new avenues of discovery. Throughout all this, Tretter's testimony seems very open and honest.

The inquest testimony offers no explanation of this sudden vacancy of the cottage. Newburgh, for example, was never even asked whether she took a walk, and no one else mentioned she did, yet she apparently was not there. In the *Boston Globe's* 1974 reinvestigation of the Chappaquiddick tragedy, she refused to account for her activities.[46]

Tretter and Keough left immediately on a second walk lasting until 2:00 A.M., looking for everyone else, they said. However, this hour or hour-and-a-half walk covered less than 0.8 mile, stopping short of the Dike Road intersection and returning when the Valiant passed them heading back to the cottage, as Tretter testified. Normally that would be a twenty- to twenty-five-minute walk. Keough accounted for the longer time by saying they had also walked "along several side roads."[47] There are three short, narrow, unpaved lanes off from Chappaquiddick Road on that stretch, but Tretter testified he was in bare feet and walked on the pavement (mentioning stepping off only when cars passed),[48] so Tretter, Keough's walking companion, apparently remained on the pavement in preference to a gravelly pathway on a pitch-black, moonless night in bare feet. If Look's much-verified time of the accident (12:45 A.M.) is used, Tretter and Keough likely met and began their walk together between 1:15 and 1:30 A.M., making the length of their walk more reasonable.

Upon their return to the cottage the second time around 2:15 A.M., they found that everyone, except of course Kennedy and Mary Jo, had miraculously rematerialized and were settling down for the night. They encountered no unusual excitement or questioning about the party's peculiar end. Tretter said he did not inquire what mission the Valiant had been on. He also testified that there were no comments or questions as to where Mary Jo was — a peculiar absence of curiosity by all.

At this time, Tretter described Gargan as looking completely normal[49] in casual wear, not wet, disheveled, agitated, or with a scraped arm (as Kennedy claimed) as he would look and act if he had just returned from diving in an unsuccessful rescue attempt of Mary Jo. (Having not planned on staying overnight, he had no change of clothes available.) Neither Gargan nor Markham mentioned any supposed rescue attempt that night, and Gargan did not mention it that morning when he revealed the accident in more detail to the young women and Tretter at the Katama Shores motel. Tretter's testimony was emphatic on this point: "He [Gargan] explained that, as I recall, that the senator had called he [sic] and Mr. Markham out of the cottage, had told them what had happened, and asked to be driven to the Edgartown Ferry. . . . He [Kennedy] just kept saying, 'Get me to Edgartown; get me to Edgartown.'"[50] This is further confirmation that the late-night rescue attempt by Gargan and Markham was simply a fabrication of Kennedy's television speech a week after the accident.

Given the strong evidence against the actuality of this second rescue attempt, the following excerpts from Tretter's testimony are intriguing. During Fernandes's questioning of Tretter on the second day, about what Gargan had told him and several of the young women at the Katama Shores motel on that Saturday morning, this exchange occurred:[51]

> Assistant District Attorney Fernandes: Did he [Gargan] mention that he had returned to the scene at all?
> Tretter: Yes.
> Fernandes: Did he say when?
> Tretter: Yes.
> Fernandes: When, what did he say?
> Tretter: Well, after, if I can just go back, after he made this —
> Judge Boyle: It would be simpler if you asked him to state all —
> Fernandes: All that was said by Mr. Gargan with reference to what had happened.

At a crucial point in midsentence, Judge Boyle interrupted Tretter, preventing him from disclosing when Gargan had returned to the accident scene. Then Tretter, in response to Fernandes's expanded question, related what Gargan had told them at the motel, quoted above: that Kennedy, after arriving back at the cottage and getting in the Valiant with Gargan and Markham, had "kept saying, 'Get me to Edgartown; get me to Edgartown.'" By quoting Gargan as denying, by clear omission, going to Dike Bridge in an immediate rescue attempt, Tretter's above testimony that Gargan said he went to the bridge at another time *confirms that Gargan visited the accident scene later in the morning, as proposed in this account.*

The questioning then wandered, with Judge Boyle interrupting Fernandes three more times as he tried to firm up the sequence of events that omitted the Gargan-Markham rescue attempt. Finally, Fernandes got back to the point where Boyle had first interrupted him, only to have Boyle interrupt him still three more times. The exchange was as follows:[52]

> Assistant District Attorney Fernandes: Do you know if anyone returned to the scene of the accident at any time after it happened?
> Judge Boyle: You mean from his personal knowledge?

Fernandes: Yes, personally.

Fernandes: Do you know or did anyone tell you that he or they returned to the scene of the incident?

Boyle: Do you mean did anyone tell him?

Fernandes: That they or anyone else returned to the scene of the accident at Dike Road and Dyke Bridge after it had occurred either immediately after or an hour or a day later, or any time after.

Boyle: Did anyone tell you that they or someone else returned to the scene of the accident, meaning the Dyke Bridge, after the accident occurred?

Tretter: Yes.

Fernandes: Who?

Tretter: Senator Kennedy in his television statement of the following week.

Fernandes: No. No one else other than Mr. Kennedy?

Tretter: That is right.

This is important but puzzling testimony. Tretter, having at first testified that Gargan told him he had returned to the accident scene and then that there had been no Gargan-Markham rescue attempt in the sequence of events during the night as related to him by Gargan, now apparently realized he had said too much, reversed himself, and denied his earlier agreement that Gargan had said he returned to Dike Bridge. A reasonable interpretation is that Tretter inferred from Judge Boyle's continual interruptions at key moments as the judge not wanting such testimony entered in the record and so complied. This is supported by the fact that this reversal in his testimony then went unexplored, and so when Gargan returned to the scene was never entered in the inquest record. Perhaps Judge Boyle saw that Fernandes was opening up Gargan's activities in a way that would further undermine Kennedy's story, and Boyle, it seemed, wished to protect Kennedy. Remember Commins's statement about the continual pressure "from Boston."

The party had come to a peculiar end, with the host, Kennedy, leaving without notice or explanation. The two cars had left during the evening on unknown missions, and only the Valiant returned. Mary Jo had disappeared. Everyone else except Crimmins had left the cottage for a time but had now returned. All but Crimmins and Markham had intended to go back to Edgartown or Katama for the night. They knew the ferry closing time and that late ferry service was available on call, and yet none of them had attempted to return by ferry, either before its normal closing time or afterward. None expressed regret or embarrassment for not returning to their comfortable, reserved motel rooms. With this extraordinarily unusual and confusing ending of the party, one would expect extensive questions and conversation at the cottage when the remaining partygoers magically reassembled there shortly after 2:00 A.M. Yet Tretter could recall no such conversation occurring, and Keough recalled only one remark by Gargan — left unexplored by the hearers — that Kennedy and Mary Jo had probably taken the ferry back to Edgartown. Nor did Markham's remark upon returning at 2:00 A.M., "You are not going to believe what happened,"[53] made in the presence of Tannenbaum and Newburgh, elicit any question, it was testified. This total lack of normal curiosity or concern that night — or was it a lack of open and full testimony at the inquest? — remains problematic.

Gargan knew at the time that his remark about Kennedy and Mary Jo's supposed return to Edgartown, just mentioned, was false, as his own testimony demonstrates. Others testified Gargan had told them that Kennedy had swum the channel and Mary Jo had driven the car across on the ferry, which Gargan also knew to be false. Gargan would have arrived back at the cottage with his mind spinning, trying to assimilate Kennedy's crash, Kennedy's setting up of his alibi by helping him across the channel, and Kennedy's expectation that he, Gargan, would report himself as a lone driver in the morning. Then he was hit with questions about where Mary Jo was. He had no idea what had happened to her at that point. That was one too many things to think about at that time. It would be best to say she was all right back at Katama, get some sleep if possible, and figure things out in the morning.

Gargan testified next at the inquest and in complete support of Kennedy's story as given in his television speech. He said he saw Kennedy leave the cottage between 11:25 and 11:30 P.M. with Mary Jo. He, like everyone else who testified seeing one or both of them leave the cottage, did not see either one get into the Olds 88 or see them drive away.

Markham, whose testimony paralleled Gargan's, did not even notice Kennedy's departure. Markham said he next saw Kennedy in the backseat of the Valiant around 12:15 to 12:30 A.M., when LaRosa called both Gargan and him out of the cottage. Gargan quoted Kennedy telling Markham and him at that time, "'The car has gone off the bridge down at the beach and Mary Jo is in it,'"[54] a statement that is inconsistent with this account. Gargan testified he immediately drove the three of them to Dike Bridge, drove across it, pointed the Valiant's headlights toward the submerged car, stripped down, jumped in the water with Markham, and tried to reach Mary Jo. However, as stated above, he did not mention this heroic rescue attempt upon returning to the cottage at 2:00 A.M. or to the remaining boiler-room gals the following morning at their motel when he finally broke the awful news of Mary Jo's drowning. Newburgh later testified that Gargan's description of the accident back at the Katama Shores motel was "something to the effect that the car went into the water, the senator was driving, and Mr. Gargan said the senator dove repeatedly to try to save her and kept repeating, 'I want you all to know that I believe it and I want you all to know that every effort possible was made to save her.'"[55] If it were true that Gargan and Markham attempted a rescue, why would Gargan not have mentioned it to such a receptive audience at that very difficult emotional moment?

Gargan's description of his and Markham's rescue attempt suffers, again, from poor questioning by District Attorney Dinis. The lateness of the revelation of this activity — in Kennedy's speech, not his police report — should have made it highly suspicious and thus in need of probing questioning of both Gargan and Markham, particularly in view of Tretter's contradictory testimony. The direction and strength of the tidal flow should have been asked, for example, as that would have helped establish the time of their activity. Also, no one requested a resolution to the contradiction between Gargan's following statements: "I reached an opening which I assumed to be one of the windows. I forced myself — I am sure it was a window, quite frankly — I got myself in."[56] Then just a few moments later, he stated, "Well, after not being able to get in through the window, I spent a period of time trying to open the doors of the car. I would say, I don't know how long I really tried to open the doors, but as I say, not being able to get in the windows, then I tried to force the doors open and I was unsuccessful."[57] Such a blatant contradiction certainly detracts from the credibility of Gargan's testimony about his supposed rescue attempt.

Following the just-quoted statement about getting in through the window of the car (but before he offered contradicting testimony), Gargan described the maneuver in detail: "I went in sidewise like this (indicating) and I got myself in and began to feel around, feeling around, feeling around. I then began to lose naturally my breath at one point and I tried to get out. I couldn't get out. I was stuck and I was stuck because I was sidewise which is, to tell you the truth, stupid, and I finally realized what the problem was and I turned myself this way (indicating) and pushed myself out and came to the top of the water." Based on what Markham would soon testify this seems to be inventive fiction rather than realistic memory. Markham, who testified he was in the water with Gargan at that time, said, "We were singularly unsuccessful in trying to get in the car,"[58] and quotes himself saying while in the water, "You know, we can't; we just can't get into the car."[59] This important contradiction of testimonies about a doubtful activity also went unexplored by Dinis and Boyle and so went unexplained, further lessening the statements' credibility.

Gargan related that after driving Kennedy to the ferry landing and after some conversation, Kennedy suddenly bolted from the car and dove in to swim to Edgartown. He was not asked why Kennedy wanted to return to Edgartown. Neither was he asked whether Kennedy was fully clothed and shod when he dove in. Gargan stated that he and Markham returned to the cottage at 2:15 A.M. to find everyone but the senator and Mary Jo. Markham testified that they returned around 2:00 A.M. and that Keough and Tretter had not yet returned. In this inconsequential discrepancy in testimony, Markham's is consistent with Keough's and Tretter's.

Apart from the above quotes from Markham's testimony, the only other significant disclosure he made was Kennedy's comment to him and Gargan the following morning when at the Chappaquiddick ferry shed making telephone calls: "I'm not going to involve you. As far as you know, you didn't know anything about the accident that night."[60] This is a firm order to participate in a cover-up. Actually, Markham testified that he had already avoided revealing any aspect of the accident to those at the cottage the previous night or early that morning.

Testimony Continues

Crimmins, next on the witness stand, supported Kennedy's story in all respects. Judge Boyle queried him at length about the use of Kennedy's Oldsmobile 88, particularly as to why he did not chauffeur Kennedy and Mary Jo to the ferry so that the car could be brought back to the cottage for use by the ten remaining partygoers. Crimmins answered simply, "I don't know. He asked me for the keys. It was his automobile and I gave them to him. I didn't question him."[61]

The situation at the time of Kennedy's departure from the cottage, as described by Crimmins, is very interesting. He testified that Kennedy called him out of the cottage and that "there were several on the lawn at the time." Crimmins saw the car leave as he returned into the cottage, though he did not see who was in it. But no one else at the party said they saw the car leave, so who were these "several" in the front yard? Neither Fernandes nor Judge Boyle then asked who they were, important information since all those who saw Kennedy and Mary Jo go out the door testified they were inside the cottage at the time. In fact, Newburgh testified that all the remaining party guests — ten of them — were inside the cottage when Kennedy and Mary Jo supposedly left together.[62] That was one more contradiction left unexplored and unexplained, lest too much be revealed.

Of course, the state police chemist, John J. McHugh, who supervised the measurement of Mary Jo's blood-alcohol level at death, was called to testify. He explained what the 0.09 percent blood-alcohol level meant: "Assuming the party is 110 pounds or thereabouts, it would be consistent with about 3.75 to 5 ounces, 80- to 90-proof liquor within one hour prior to death. Now let me put that another way. It could result from that or it could result into higher amounts of liquor over a period of two hours prior to death."[63] Thus, if she left the party only a few minutes before the accident at 12:50 A.M., this indicates she imbibed three or four drinks in the previous hour, but if she left around 11:30 P.M., as several testified, and she died at about 12:50 A.M. (or later by the air-bubble theory), one is forced to conclude she had more than that after 10:30 P.M. That is surprisingly heavy drinking by Mary Jo, but why else would she have searched out the backseat of Kennedy's car for a "snooze"? And remember, as trial lawyers like to say, "Circumstantial evidence doesn't lie; only people do."

Alcohol intake was naturally a persistent subject of questioning at the inquest. If the admitted number of drinks by each of the party guests is added, along with two for Tretter, for whom the question was forgotten, and taking the minimum of three for Mary Jo from her blood-alcohol level, the twelve partygoers had a modest total of twenty-one drinks. If we assign a jigger of liquor (1.5 ounces) to each drink except those drunk by Kennedy, who admitted to 2-ounce drinks, we conclude that about 33 ounces of liquor were consumed. From Crimmins's testimony of the amount of liquor he brought to the party and the amount he carried away, three-quarters of a half-gallon of vodka, a fifth of scotch, and a quart and a half of rum were consumed, for a total of 122 ounces of liquor.[64] (Nance Lyons confirmed seeing three and a half empties the morning after the party.)[65] From that estimate, about 6 ounces should be subtracted for the four drinks that Crimmins likely had from the supply on Wednesday and Thursday evenings, leaving the consumption at the party at 116 ounces of liquor. And added to that should be the amount of beer drunk, to which no one admitted. Crimmins testified that a half-case was consumed. Since beer is typically 5 percent alcohol, twelve cans of beer are equivalent to 17 ounces of liquor (85 proof). The total equivalent consumption is thus 133 ounces of liquor, which is *four times* the admitted amount consumed and well over 10 ounces of liquor per party guest.

This rough — but testimony-based — calculation proves that the cookout involved heavy drinking. The excess over admitted intake was likely uneven among partygoers. Gargan described LaRosa, for example, as a very light drinker. On the other hand, Kennedy had a reputation of heavy drinking, so he likely led the way. With this amount of alcohol consumption established, the level of raucous noise heard at the neighboring Silva cottage and the gaiety-induced missing of the last ferry are certainly understandable — as is doing a hootchy-kootchy dance down the centerline of Chappaquiddick Road. Still more to the point, overly fast, inattentive driving under the influence was highly likely.

The first of the young women to testify was Esther Rose Newburgh (inquest spelling; *Newberg* in many other publications), perhaps because she had acted as a spokesperson for the boiler-room girls during the media frenzy in the days following the accident. The *New York Times* interviewed her five days after the tragedy and wrote, "Miss Newberg described it as an informal group, with no one keeping particular track of who was there or who wasn't there at any given time. Thus, she said, no one specifically missed either the Senator or Miss Kopechne or noticed what time they had left."[66] Contrast this with her sworn inquest testimony six months later:[67]

> Assistant District Attorney Fernandes: Prior to his leaving did you become aware that Mr. Kennedy left at a certain point?
> Newburgh: Yes.
> Fernandes: Can you tell us when?
> Newburgh: 11:30.
> Fernandes: What makes you say 11:30?
> Newburgh: I have a rather large watch that I wear all the time and I looked at it.

Moments later in her testimony, she continued with more specific memories contrary to her press statement:

> Fernandes: Well, where were you when you saw him [Kennedy] leave?
> Newburgh: In the living room.
> Fernandes: Where was he?

Newburgh: At the door. The screen door was open. I saw him walk out.

Fernandes: Out of the living room?

Newburgh: That is right.

Fernandes: And were you able to tell whether he was alone or not?

Newburgh: Miss Kopechne was directly behind him.

When Newburgh was recalled to the stand two days later (concerning an irrelevant rumor), she again emphatically contradicted her comment to the press in July:[68]

Judge Boyle: And you saw her [Mary Jo] the time she left?

Newburgh: Exactly the time she left.

Nance Lyons and Cricket Keough testified similarly about Kennedy and Mary Jo leaving, and Susan Tannenbaum remembered Mary Jo leaving at that time. Maryellen Lyons, though not seeing either leave the cottage, realized they were both gone by 11:20 P.M. (However, none saw either of them get into, or leave in, a car.) Was this unanimous and precise support for Kennedy's timing of events a striking example of "recovered memory," or was it the result of "preparation" for the inquest by the lawyers arranged and paid for by Kennedy?

This memory about Kennedy and Mary Jo's departure stands out in the long questioning of Newburgh as the only specific thing she "remembered." And much else of her testimony did not seem to meet the test of common sense. She did not find it peculiar that Mary Jo, her roommate at the Katama Shores, left without so much as a word to her. Newburgh said the young women all intended to return to that motel for the night and knew the ferry schedule and its possible late service, but she offered no convincing reason why they missed the ferry. She did not find it disturbing or even particularly unusual that Gargan and Markham drove off from the party for an extended period. When Gargan returned, plopped onto the couch next to Newburgh, and said, "I am exhausted. If you knew what I had been through, you would let me lie there," it did not arouse any questioning by Newburgh.[69] After Gargan claimed that night that Kennedy had swum the channel back to

Edgartown, Newburgh testified she still imagined Mary Jo had driven across on the ferry to the motel. With that juxtaposition, Judge Boyle, who had taken over with rapid-fire questions at Newburgh, let out an incredulous, "That she had driven and he swam?"[70]

After Peachey testified about encountering Kennedy at 2:25 A.M. outside the Shiretown Inn, already described in chapter 2, George Kennedy, the supervisor of the Oak Bluffs office of the Registry of Motor Vehicles was called to the stand. He testified to the skid marks on the bridge, the gouges in the rub rail, and various measurements of the bridge. His response to the most important question, the speed of Kennedy's car, was simply nonsensical. After stating his opinion that the speed was twenty to twenty-two miles per hour, George Kennedy explained, "All right, a car operating at twenty miles per hour has a reaction time of any person operating approximately three-quarters of a second before a person removes his foot from the gas and applies the brake. Approximately at twenty miles an hour the vehicle would move approximately twenty-two feet in the three-quarters of a second for the reaction time. Then a vehicle, after the brakes have been applied at twenty miles an hour, then the vehicle should stop in twenty-five feet. Now, there is a distance of twenty-five, twenty-two, forty-seven feet."[71] That has no relevance to the skid mark of thirty-three feet on the bridge with the possibility of additional, unobserved skid marks in the gravel before the bridge, and it does not even consider the significant launch speed of the car plunging off the bridge for thirty-some feet.

One is left totally perplexed at the complete incoherence and apparent idiocy of Inspector Kennedy's testimony and then the total lack of expected questions needed to clarify his determination of the speed of the Kennedy car, a key question of the entire inquest. What was going on here? The transcript offers a hint: it shows seven interruptions of Inspector Kennedy's testimony by Judge Boyle, each to have discussion off the record. In their book, the Tedrows offer an answer:

> Here is what we were told about the inquest speed situation. The Registry of Motor Vehicles of Massachusetts offered evidence at the inquest to show that the car was going 35 to 40 miles per hour at the time,

but Judge Boyle would not accept it. The proceedings were stopped, the parties went off the record, and the Judge stated he would not allow evidence of speed more than 20 to 22 miles an hour. The Registry witness gave evidence on that basis. The Judge not only ruled against evidence of a higher (more truthful) speed but actually had the references to it physically expunged from the record.[72]

If true, this is damning evidence of Judge Boyle's bias, his not wanting complete information on the accident, and his intention to protect Kennedy. Unfortunately, the Tedrows do not reference the source of this information (they do not give specific sources for anything in their book), but it is hard to imagine an alternative explanation for Inspector Kennedy's testimony being left in such an incoherent and nonsensical form. Inspector Kennedy, Fernandes, and Boyle were not that dumb: something else was going on, so the Tedrows' explanation seems believable. It also fits with Boyle's secretary Commins relating the continual "communications and directions coming down from Boston to Judge Boyle to control the whole procedure."

Deputy Sheriff Look was next to testify. Under questioning he related his chance, but crucial, encounter with Kennedy's car before it took off on Dike Road, as described fully earlier. Thus the only aspect of Look's testimony worth mentioning here was Judge Boyle's nitpicking attempt to undermine Look's identification of the car because he could not be "more definite about its color other than it was a dark color"[73] and because he had observed only the first and last numbers of its license plate. Boyle's questioning to undermine Look's testimony appears as an attempt to support Kennedy's timing of the accident.

Mortician Frieh followed Look to the stand. Frieh described how he was called to the accident scene, witnessed Mills's short examination of the body, took the body to his funeral home, awaited a decision on an autopsy, cleansed and embalmed the body, observed no injuries beyond a scrape of a left knuckle, took a blood sample, and arranged with the Kielty Funeral Home in Plymouth, Pennsylvania, for air delivery of the body on the following day. The only notable information was his answer to Fernandes's question of what he observed when Mills pressed on the chest and abdominal areas of the body. Frieh stated, "It produced some water flow, water and foam, mostly foam."[74] This was the first testimony of significant air in the lungs, rather than water-filled lungs typical of drowning victims. This seemed like the perfect testimony to introduce the suffocation observations of Farrar, who was next to testify.

Farrar's testimony was crisply professional, describing his recovery of the body, its configuration, and its location in the car. He testified he first saw the sandal-clad feet of the body through the submerged rear window. The body, hard and stiff with rigor mortis, had its head cocked backward to place the nose at the highest possible point in the foot well where a pocket of air was initially trapped. The hands were grasping the seat-cushion edge to hold that position, and the legs were extended toward the rear window. He extracted the body carefully past the remaining sharp edges of the blown-out, right-rear window.

In support of the foot-well air pocket, a crucial part of his suffocation hypothesis, Farrar continued, "I was partially on the surface and partially under the water and at the time it [Kennedy's car] was righted I observed large air bubbles and [also] at the time it was being towed out, emanating from the vehicle."[75] However, in his final report on the inquest, Judge Boyle stated, "Testimony was not *sought or allowed* concerning how long Kopechne might have lived, had such a condition [foot-well air pocket] existed"[76] (emphasis added). What is going on here? How could Boyle miss this contrary statement? It seems likely that he was simply careless in his expunging of testimony that he did not want in the record because it would undermine or contradict his desired findings. Certainly Farrar would have mentioned the body's partial buoyancy as he moved it through the water and its failure to sink from its recovered position in the car, as it would have with water-filled lungs. Absence of these facts suggests expunging of this testimony.

In his book, Kappel reports, "Farrar stated to investigator Robert Cutler in 1971 that 'the stenographer's tape was torn up when Boyle ordered most of the testimony [Farrar's] about bubbles bursting around the car stricken from the record.'"[77] Farrar affirmed this statement that he made to Cutler to the author, offering more detail: "When I testified about the time I thought Mary Jo could have survived based on my belief she suffocated, Judge Boyle said, 'Strike that from the record.' As the court stenographer put a line through that testimony, Judge Boyle said, 'No, tear that out of the record and give it to me,' which she did. Judge Boyle then tore that transcript of testimony into small pieces as I watched. He simply tried to belittle me."[78] This makes Farrar's comments and demeanor upon leaving the inquest following his testimony a little puzzling. As he emerged from the courthouse into a sea of reporters and TV cameras, Farrar told them, as quoted in Sherrill's book, "'We are satisfied we had the opportunity to give everything we had to offer,'"[79] and went on to state that Dinis's questioning was "'very fair and very thorough.'" How could Farrar say this if he had just seen Judge Boyle actually tear up his testimony? Farrar has told the author he felt intimidated, was sworn to secrecy as to what had happened, and was unsure of what, if any, right he had to challenge Judge Boyle, so he just decided to put a good face on the situation. This is thus Boyle's second expunging of testimony, his second editing of the truth, his second biased protection of Kennedy.

Farrar also testified about his examination of the recovered car, an activity that the police apparently failed to do adequately. He described the driver's-side window as "rolled down to an inch of the bottom," the driver's door locked, the two windows on the passenger's side shattered inward, the ignition switch on, the lights on high beam, the gear in drive, and the brake off.[80] He also had recovered, from the bottom of the channel close to the wreck, the chrome strip that broke loose from the right side of the car when it first hit the water. This allowed him to measure the distance the car had plunged off the bridge as thirty-six feet from the center body gouge in the rub rail. He also found that the drop to the water was eight feet from the launch point. (The tidal differences in this height measured around 10:30 A.M. before low tide and the accident time at 12:50 A.M. after low tide should be a small part of a foot.) The launch point was from a section of the bridge with an incline of 8.8 percent (five degrees),[81] but the car went at an angle of twenty-seven degrees to the upward slope. Thus, it is accurate enough to take the upward launch angle as four degrees above horizontal.

Newton's Second Law of dynamics predicts that a body launched at an upward angle with an initial speed follows a parabolic trajectory under the influence of gravity. With the three data just given (the launch angle, distance dropped, and distance of horizontal air travel), a simple calculation[82] finds that the car plunged off the bridge at 30.3 miles per hour. To this, of course, must be added the decrease in speed from skidding some thirty-three feet on the bridge (and possibly some additional feet on the gravel approach) in order to find the approach speed of the car. The sum would seem to approach the 40 miles per hour estimated by the Registry (but disallowed at the inquest). That is about double Kennedy's claimed speed, but if his perception was poor enough not to see a bridge ahead, why would anyone believe he was aware of a speedometer reading of 20 miles per hour at the time?

The Boiler-Room Girls

Maryellen Lyons was the next of the young women to testify. She related taking two walks with LaRosa, consistent with his description. She spoke of speculation that Kennedy walked back to the cottage because his car was stuck in the sand somewhere. She pointed out that Gargan and Markham, upon their return, appeared very normal and discouraged most questions as to what had been happening. However, she testified that Gargan had told them that they had been down to the ferry slip looking for a boat, that Kennedy had dove in and swum the channel, and that they had gone in the water after him, supposedly worried about Kennedy's bad back — an activity that Tretter said Gargan spoke of at the Katama Shores the next morning. How they could appear completely normal to Maryellen, rather than sopping wet, was left unexplained. She also testified that Gargan said that Mary Jo had taken the last ferry with Kennedy's car and was back at Katama. When Judge Boyle asked whether hearing of Mary Jo taking the ferry by car and of Kennedy swimming across the channel struck her as unusual, Maryellen replied, "No. Not really, Your Honor."[83] One can picture again the consternation on Boyle's face at that moment.

Perhaps Maryellen gave the best explanation for the passive, unquestioning acceptance of all the peculiar, late-party happenings and conversation when she said, "Well, no one was concerned about anything."[84] That would seem to characterize a collective, happy, relaxed, and fuzzy state of inebriation, along with late-night sleepiness. Also, the several walks that the partygoers took late that night suggest efforts "to walk it off."

Nance Lyons, Maryellen's sister, seems to have been the most forthcoming in her testimony among the young women, though at the time she was a legislative aide to Senator Kennedy. She was a close friend of Mary Jo and had previously roomed with her in Washington for three years. Perhaps she felt a greater willingness to be open, in hopes of helping to understand the death of her close friend. Nance Lyons said she saw Kennedy and Mary Jo leave the cottage before 11:30 P.M. but, without a watch, was uncertain of the time. She did not see them go anywhere after leaving the cottage but thought it was unusual that neither spoke to anyone before leaving. She agreed with Newburgh's testimony that the party continued unabated after Kennedy and Mary Jo's departure, with talking, singing, and drinking. Nance Lyons also said "the party continued normally for a period of time" even after Gargan and Markham left, which by Look's reliable timing was well after 1:00 A.M.[85] Thus her testimony seems roughly consistent with Dodie Silva's observation that the party noise did not abate until 1:30 A.M. Lyons offered no convincing reason why they had all missed the last ferry. She confirmed the walk with her sister and LaRosa on which they encountered Look but was unsure of the time. Her belief that it was after Gargan and Markham had left would appear to be confusion. She also said that Gargan, upon his return, had convinced them that Kennedy had swum the channel and that Mary Jo had driven across on the ferry to her motel. On his third hearing of this nonsense, Judge Boyle did not bother to express his incredulity.

Nance Lyons's most significant testimony supports the events as told here in chapter 2. The essence of her testimony is that she was convinced that Gargan did not know the complete story of the accident — its real tragedy of Mary Jo's death — at 2:00 A.M. but did later that morning. The questioning was as follows:[86]

Assistant District Attorney Fernandes: You say it was fairly obvious when he [Gargan] came back to pick you up that morning that something had transpired by the expression on his face.

Nance Lyons: Yes, sir.

Fernandes: When you saw him or had that conversation with him that night when he returned from trying to get a boat, did you make any observation of him?

Lyons: No, sir. In retrospect I could compare the two and say that *it appeared when he returned [at 2:00 A.M.] that he had no knowledge of what had actually transpired.* (emphasis added)

Fernandes: And you felt something was wrong by what observations or what appearances or what in fact made you conclude that something was wrong?

Lyons: When he returned in the morning?

Fernandes: Other than what he said, yes.

Lyons: Just his face.

Rosemary Keough followed Nance Lyons on the witness stand. She testified she had two scotch-and-waters during the party, danced with Tretter and Gargan, backed "the party line" by recalling both Kennedy and Mary Jo leaving around 11:20 P.M., and had no conversation with either as they departed.

Her testimony about her later activities is most important. She said she looked at Tannenbaum's watch at 11:40 P.M. (an unusual but convenient observation to establish her presence in the cottage after the time she testified that Kennedy left), stepped out of the cottage and sat for a quarter-hour or so (no companion mentioned), and then left on a forty-five-minute to an hour walk in the direction of the ferry.[87] Moments later, she corrected her estimate of the time of leaving on the walk as between 12:15 and 12:30 A.M. She said she was with Tretter on the walk *but did not say they left on the walk together.* Their return to the cottage was somewhere between 1:00 and 1:15 A.M., she stated.

Interestingly, she could not testify as to how many cars were at the cottage when she left, even though she would have had to walk past or around the white Valiant between the cottage and the road. Of course, if she did not participate in that part of the walk, as suggested earlier, a noncommittal answer was the safest answer, particularly if she had, as offered here, gotten into the Olds 88 with Kennedy.

We interpreted Tretter's testimony earlier as indicating that Tretter began his walk past the Valiant alone, and we reasoned from the events he described that he had had to encounter Kennedy and his front-seat companion walking back from the crash scene. A careful reading of Tretter's testimony revealed he switched from describing his walk at its beginning in first-person singular "I" to first-person plural "we" after the time when he had to have encountered Kennedy and his front-seat companion returning from the accident. All testimony agrees that the "we" refers to Keough and Tretter on the walk. Thus, we concluded that it was at this point that Keough joined him on the walk, and so Keough was Kennedy's front-seat companion (recall that no one arrived back at the cottage with Kennedy).

Keough's correcting herself on the timing of the first walk is interesting. She had had over five months to collect and review her memory and prepare her testimony. She gave other times with certainty. It is hard to believe she was suddenly mixed up, and she certainly was not thinking about those times for the first time at the inquest. Her testimony at the point of correction does not show tension or confusion. In fact, her interruption of Dinis to correct herself smacks of being planned. Why? If she did not begin this walk with Tretter, as reasoned earlier, it might turn out helpful to have the time rather uncertain, if contradictions in testimony were to arise concerning the beginning.

The questioning of Keough was as strikingly inadequate as that of Tretter concerning their first walk — perhaps more so since Dinis had had two more days to ponder Tretter's testimony. Keough was not asked about any encounters with people or vehicles during the walk, even those mentioned by Tretter. Dinis's and Judge Boyle's inability to simply relate events, times, and places must be described as either inattentive, inept, or intentional. It was disastrous to the fact-finding success of the inquest.

Keough testified that, upon returning to the cottage after the first walk, she and Tretter found no one there (Crimmins would have been unobserved, sleeping in a bedroom) and so immediately left on another, longer walk, again in the direction of the ferry, "to look for the rest of the people."[88] Keough testified that they did not find any of them and returned around 2:00 A.M. to the cottage to find everyone back there — magically — except for Kennedy and Mary Jo. Just as during Tretter's testimony, how these puzzling movements occurred was left unexplored once again.

Tretter's testimony is crucial to unraveling Keough's movements throughout that night. Recall that he testified that she rode with him in the Kennedy car to get a radio for the party. However, Dodie Silva observed no passenger in the passing car, bringing into question Keough's presence in it. Three of the partygoers, LaRosa, Crimmins, and Kennedy, testified either that Tretter drove Kennedy's Olds 88 or specifically that he took it to borrow a radio, yet none mentioned Keough's riding with him. But, typical of the inept questioning, none of them were quizzed about whether she did accompany Tretter on his errand. It was on that ride when she claimed she left her handbag in the car, which was later found on the front-seat compartment ceiling of the overturned car submerged in Poucha Pond. And her explanation of not retrieving it in the nearly three hours after returning to the cottage seems weak. It was argued earlier that, if it had actually been left there then, anyone other than Keough getting in to ride with Kennedy would have immediately taken the misplaced handbag into the cottage to its owner. Tretter could not corroborate, when asked at the inquest, anything concerning the handbag.

Any inference of Keough not being the front-seat companion with Kennedy on the fateful ride to Dike Bridge — never explicitly requested during the inquest — rests entirely on Tretter. He testified she accompanied him on the walks that occurred during the crucial two-hour time period of the tragedy. No one else offered testimony in support of Tretter's statements, and none was requested. *The inquest record is devoid of third-party testimony of Keough's movements during those crucial hours of the party.* Did anyone see her leave the cottage? Did she leave with Kennedy? Did anyone see her leave on a walk with Tretter, which his wording denied? Did anyone notice any scratches, bruises, or dicing on her right shoulder or face late that night, which likely marked the front-seat companion? No one was asked these or related questions at the inquest. Thus Tretter never had to give his testimony within any context of Keough being somehow involved in the accident.

It should also be remembered that, while Keough testified she was away from the party for the key two hours encompassing the accident and its aftermath, Newburgh, apparently sensing early — or knowing? — that Keough needed an alibi, offered a diametrically opposite alibi to the press for Keough, saying that she had never left the party.

The final testimony received at the inquest was from Susan Tannenbaum. She was the least forthcoming of all the witnesses and added nothing of significance to the record. One can see in her testimony a determination to reveal as little as possible, as she used a simple "yes" or "no" sixty-three times and "I don't know" and "not that I remember" many times. Her lack of cooperation is exemplified by her claim of not remembering even being told how Mary Jo died![89]

Of course, testimony was also received during the inquest from Arena, Peachey, Mills, the ferrymen, and others, but because their activities and observations have been fully recorded in earlier chapters or alluded to in regard to others' testimony, their testimonies need not be rehashed here.

On the other hand, it is worth noting that several relevant witnesses were not called. Mrs. Sylvia Malm, who left the outdoor light on through the night at Dyke House on that moonless night, was not called. Neither was her daughter Sylvia, who read until midnight near an open window facing Dike Bridge and heard no splash into Poucha Pond before turning in. Stan Moore was not called to describe those important moments on the Shiretown Inn deck when Gargan and Markham's arrival changed Kennedy's demeanor from relaxed and sociable to shocked and grim. Ross Richards's wife also was not called to testify on the same aspect. None of the Silva family, who endured the party noise from the neighboring Lawrence cottage and heard it continue long after most of the partygoers claimed, was called. And, in particular, Dodie Silva was not called to the stand to testify that she had seen a man (Tretter) driving toward the ferry (on his errand to find a radio for the party) with no one else visible in the car, key information that would have undermined Keough's testimony about her misplaced handbag. Jon Ahlbum, the wrecker driver who could have testified about the large bubbles of air (or oxygen-depleted exhalation) that came up as he righted Kennedy's car in the water, was not called. Equally significantly, no witness was recalled (except the irrelevant recall of Newburgh) to clarify the many contradictions revealed in the testimony or to fill the many gaps revealed by a study of the transcript of the proceedings. But after three and a half days of testimony, Judge Boyle determined he had heard enough, the inquest was concluded, and he began his perusal of the transcript and preparation of a report.

Judge Boyle's Report

Judge Boyle filed his report with the Superior Court of Suffolk County on February 18. The Supreme Judicial Court's impoundment decision of the previous fall restricted its access to the attorney general, the district attorney, and relevant lawyers. Though it would be more than another month before the report's contents would become public, it was and would become known as both a bomb and a dud!

Judge Boyle's report began with definitions of places and things and then presented a 2,500-word summary of the happenings based on his view of the combined testimony. He admitted that the testimony "is not wholly consistent," a woeful understatement, but dismissed the contradictions as minor.[90] Boyle stated he had disallowed testimony on the air-bubble hypothesis, as was discussed earlier. Whether Boyle was influenced by the rejection of Farrar's testimony on the air-bubble and suffocation issue at the exhumation and autopsy hearing in Pennsylvania or by Farrar's many zealous public statements is not known, but the latter seems more likely. In the end it was just one more prejudicial error of omission on Boyle's part.

Judge Boyle stated his duty: "The statute states that I must report the name of any person whose unlawful act or negligence *appears* to have contributed to Kopechne's death" (Boyle's emphasis). Then he quoted a Massachusetts precedent: "'It [an inquest] is designed merely to ascertain facts for the purpose of subsequent prosecution' and ' . . . the investigating judge may himself issue process against a person whose probable guilt is disclosed.'"[91] He said he would use the standard of "probable guilt" rather than the more stringent standard of "proof beyond a reasonable doubt" used in criminal trials. He further explained he would "draw inferences known as presumption of facts," which he cited as "'nothing more than a probable or natural explanation of facts . . . and arises from the commonly accepted experiences of mankind and the inferences which reasonable men would draw from experiences.'"

Following that prologue, Judge Boyle gave his list of twelve facts and then dropped his first bomb: "I infer a reasonable and probable explanation of the totality of the above facts is that Kennedy and Kopechne did *not* intend to return to Edgartown at that time; that Kennedy did *not* intend to drive to the ferry slip and his turn onto Dike Road was intentional."[92] In short, *Judge Boyle disbelieved the salient claims of Kennedy's whole story.*

Then opining that Dike Bridge was a traffic hazard, Judge Boyle wrote, "A speed of even twenty miles an hour, as Kennedy testified to, operating a car as large as this Oldsmobile, would at least be negligent and, possibly, reckless. If Kennedy knew of this hazard, his operation of the vehicle constituted criminal conduct."[93] Citing Kennedy's traversal of Dike Bridge twice the previous afternoon, Judge Boyle went on, "I believe it probable that Kennedy knew of the hazard that lay ahead of him on Dike Road but that, for some reason not apparent from the testimony, he failed to exercise due caution as he approached the bridge." After this incomplete syllogism, which we will return to momentarily, Boyle declared, "I, therefore, find there is probable cause to believe that Edward M. Kennedy operated his motor vehicle negligently on a way or in a place to which the public have a right of access and that such operation appears to have contributed to the death of Mary Jo Kopechne." Boyle had dropped his second bomb: *Kennedy's negligence contributed to Mary Jo's death!*

This was the outcome most feared by the Kennedy legal team, because in Massachusetts, such a finding normally led automatically to an involuntary manslaughter charge. But Judge Boyle then abjectly failed to follow the instructions for his role as he had quoted them at the opening of the inquest: "The primary object of an inquest is to ascertain the facts to decide the question of whether or not criminal proceedings shall be instituted against the person or persons responsible for the death." In his report, he had made it more incumbent on himself to act when he quoted a Massachusetts Supreme Judicial Court decision that stated, "The investigating judge may himself issue process against a person whose *probable* guilt is disclosed." But he failed to take that next demanded step: charge Kennedy with involuntary manslaughter. Boyle, who retired hastily the day following release of his report, chose to leave office with a cowering whimper, not a courageous action and not even a perfunctory exercise of his duty. Thus he dropped a dud, not a third bomb.

Why Boyle fled his judgeship at that moment, while in good health and just sixty-three years old, will never be known, but the timing was so striking that it clamors for an explanation, even if only speculative. His son, James A. Boyle, Jr., said his father never mentioned "a word to us about it [the inquest]" throughout his later life.[94] Normally one could expect a retired judge who had presided over a nationally recognized proceedings to express some pride in his handling of it, enjoy reminiscence about a key questioning or wise ruling, remark on an unexpected revelation, or comment on the reasoning of his conclusions. But Judge Boyle did none of these. Why? Previously we reported he had been under intense and improper pressure "from Boston" throughout the inquest, according to his secretary Commins. Thus his disallowance, even expunging, of testimony to protect Kennedy, which was so inconsistent with his reputation for fairness and honesty, can only be understood as resulting from phoned threats, not procedural or judicial advice. That could well explain his rather protective stance in questioning Kennedy, in his disallowance of George Kennedy's car-speed testimony, in his attempt to undermine Deputy Look's identification of Kennedy's car, in his disallowance of Farrar's suffocation testimony, and in his obstructive role in Tretter's testimony. However, in the end Boyle could not in good conscience ignore the mound of evidence against Kennedy and felt forced to find that he had given false testimony and was negligent in causing Mary Jo's death. But Boyle's courage failed him when it came to following his own expressed duty of issuing process against anyone likely guilty of such negligence. Boyle couldn't be proud of his conflicted and timid behavior. More likely, he felt shame. Silence was his only way of handling it.

Let us return to Judge Boyle's incomplete syllogism. He stated his major premise as: "If Kennedy knew of this hazard, his operation of the vehicle constituted criminal conduct." Then, sandwiched in much verbiage, Boyle gave the minor premise as: "Kennedy knew of the hazard." Logic then demands the conclusion that Kennedy's operation of the vehicle constituted criminal conduct. Apparently Boyle did not dare to complete his own syllogism, because such a direct statement of Kennedy's "criminal conduct" would then, Boyle must have felt, force his own hand to issue an involuntary manslaughter charge, an action he obviously dared not take. So he used words that implied this conclusion without saying it openly. Once again, Massachusetts justice chose coddling, rather than evenhandedness, for a powerful senator.

District Attorney Dinis was not constrained by Judge Boyle's timidity. Dinis still had the power to pursue an indictment against Kennedy and now had all the independent justification he could possibly ask for. But Dinis had done everything he could for seven months to avoid doing just that. He was running for reelection in 1970 on the Democratic ticket with Kennedy. Trying Kennedy for involuntary manslaughter during their reelection campaigns would have certainly ended both of their political careers. And with Boyle's report impounded and thus its impact unknown to the public, there was no new pressure on Dinis to do his duty. So just like Boyle, he chose to duck his duty — even after Boyle's report became public.

The legal machinery had come to a standstill, the investigation was in a state of suspended animation, and the inquest testimony was impounded for a time. With both Judge Boyle and District Attorney Dinis sitting on their hands, the public was left wondering what had happened.

There had been demands for a grand jury investigation of the Chappaquiddick accident from the start. Now it seemed to the jury's foreman, Les Leland, that the grand jury was the only means left to get to the bottom of what the public overwhelmingly regarded as a cover-up. Leland had learned that not just the district attorney, but the foreman also, could initiate grand jury proceedings.

Leland swung into action.

Chapter 9

The Grand Jury

Just two months before the Chappaquiddick tragedy, a new Dukes County Grand Jury had been impaneled in Edgartown for a year's term. The last of the twenty names drawn from the drum of eligible jurors was Leslie H. Leland, who became the elected foreman at the jury's first meeting. The disappointing saga of the grand jury's efforts to investigate the Chappaquiddick tragedy is a personal account of Leland's frustrations in confronting a Massachusetts justice system that appeared to him determined to protect Kennedy, a story that Leland recently described in a book with Jerry Shaffer, *Left to Die*.

Leland, a twenty-nine-year-old pharmacist, owned Leslie's Drug Store on Main Street in Vineyard Haven, the commercial-port town of Martha's Vineyard. He had graduated from the Massachusetts College of Pharmacy in Boston in 1963 and purchased his own pharmacy, previously run by his grandparents, just a year before Kennedy's accident. Founding his own business made him a very busy man, but he was young and energetic, vigorous in personality, and took his foreman's duties very seriously. But, typical of grand jurors, he had no training in law, and he was rather naive about the political machinations — aren't we all? — that can intrude in the justice system. In the nine months following Kennedy's accident, Leland received a very unpleasant education in these matters.

Leland, as grand jury foreman, was not immune to the publicity storm that enveloped Martha's Vineyard immediately following the news of Kennedy's automobile accident, Mary Jo Kopechne's death, and the Chappaquiddick party. "What was the grand jury going to do?" the media people asked repeatedly. Leland had no answer. His short experience with the workings of the grand jury had taught him that it was a deliberative body that judged whether information presented to it by District Attorney Dinis justified issuing a bill of indictment. The initiative for any indictment came from the D.A. who had done the investigation and ran the grand jury's proceedings. Leland was unaware of any of the foreman's legal powers, beyond chairing deliberations and reporting their results.

Thus Leland's meeting held a few days following Kennedy's accident with Chief Arena and Special Prosecutor Steele, described earlier, in which they attempted to influence Leland's thinking by the subterfuge of talking between themselves (hopefully to avoid any charge of jury tampering) was surprising, puzzling, and intimidating to Leland. The message was certainly clear: there was no need for a grand jury investigation of a simple automobile accident. But why was it directed at him? At that point, Leland had no understanding that as foreman he could initiate and even manage a grand jury investigation.

Leland naturally turned to Dinis for information and counsel. Dinis confirmed what media people had told Leland: he did have the power to initiate a grand jury investigation into the Chappaquiddick tragedy. In fact, for a time following the accident, Dinis encouraged him to do so. But at that point, with no legal experience beyond his short tenure as jury foreman, Leland was understandably reluctant to jump into the national limelight of a politically charged investigation. And why was Dinis not initiating the investigation himself? It was his duty as district attorney, Leland thought.

Leland was just an honest, conscientious citizen caught up in the scandal by the luck of his name being drawn from the drum. But he took his accidental involvement seriously, and he, like the vast majority of citizens, felt that a cover-up was occurring. He wanted to do the job thrust upon him as well as he could, and the media's insistence on a full investigation kept the pressure on him. As the days passed with Dinis initiating no grand jury proceedings, Leland contacted the Massachusetts attorney general, Robert H. Quinn, to ask him about the foreman's powers in this regard. Quinn told Leland, "It's up to the attorney general, a district attorney or a judge."[1] That legally wrong advice — contrary to what Dinis had told him — left Leland quite understandably in a state of confusion. Was Quinn that mistaken, or was he just trying to protect Kennedy from a grand jury investigation? Or was Dinis wrong? Indecision resulted.

Dinis did not want the political onus on him for initiating a grand jury investigation — he was up for reelection the following year. But feeling the pressure to do "something" after the Kennedy television speech, Dinis announced an inquest would be held to determine the facts from the participants under oath, as described earlier. With this action and Dinis's assurance that he would keep Leland informed about the inquest, Leland felt the pressure ease.

Leland marked time impatiently, as the inquest was held in early January of 1970 and Judge Boyle wrote his report on it in February. Those records, as discussed earlier, were impounded, and their contents were unknown to Leland. Leland did not know that Boyle had found Kennedy negligent in Mary Jo's death, but he could see that Dinis took no legal action whatsoever as a result of the inquest. Leland, marshaling a medley of metaphors, expressed his exasperation: "There's been a whitewash, a cover-up, and things have been swept under the rug."[2] He felt strongly that a grand jury investigation was the last chance for justice to be served. With unanimous support from the other grand jurors, he wrote Chief Justice G. Joseph Tauro of the Superior Court on March 17 requesting that the grand jury be called out of recess to investigate the Chappaquiddick accident. When a television newsperson heard of the letter and contacted the Superior Court, a spokesperson denied its receipt until it was learned Leland would exhibit the return receipt in a television interview.[3] It was then belatedly acknowledged. Was this attempted Kennedy protection?

But that was far from the worst that Leland would be subjected to. Shortly after calling for the grand jury to be convened, he received a phone call in the morning at his pharmacy from a crude, male voice with an underworld parlance threatening his wife and children with harm unless he called off the grand jury investigation.[4] It was frightening and intimidating. But was it a real threat or just a crank call? Leland was not sure. He decided not to tell his wife, or anyone else, about it. He would press ahead.

But a few days later he received another call, this one at home in the evening, from a more cultured voice. This man made it clear he was reiterating the previous threat, referring to the first caller as "my friend" and implying that person was the enforcer. Leland was really shaken this time. It was not a crank call; it was a serious, coordinated threat. He talked it over with his wife. She counseled him to abandon the grand jury investigation and let Kennedy go scot-free. But Leland regarded himself as the only white knight left standing on the field of battle against Kennedy's dark forces, and the evasions and frustrations Leland had already endured in the previous eight months had toughened his resolve. He was determined to go forward, but not without police protection. He called the state police, who readily agreed to give his family around-the-clock protective surveillance. When a week later a letter arrived renewing the same threats, the police intensified their efforts. Since a grand jury indictment was a peril only for Kennedy, who else besides someone in the Kennedy camp would have been behind those threats?

Chief Justice Tauro, forced to acknowledge that reconvening the grand jury had been requested by the foreman, not by the district attorney, granted the request and scheduled its reconvening for April 6. He assigned Judge Wilfred J. Paquet, an avid Kennedy admirer, to preside over the grand jury's deliberations in the Dukes County Courthouse in Edgartown. Dinis had told Leland that the grand jury would find the inquest testimony and Judge Boyle's report quite interesting. That clearly indicated to Leland that the grand jury would have access to the testimony, as would be expected for a secret, judicial, investigative body with power to issue subpoenas and indictments. Leland, tired of Dinis's vacillation and forked tongue, planned to conduct the grand jury investigation and questioning himself, using Dinis only as legal counsel.

Judge Paquet, hearing of Leland's plan from his public statements, began his intimidation and obstruction of the grand jury by letting it be known (through Dinis) that Paquet was considering holding Leland in contempt of court, supposedly for talking too much in public. Though Paquet did not follow through on so arbitrary an action, he began the proceedings by improperly allowing a Roman Catholic priest from the local church to offer a prayer from the bench "that prejudice be set aside and replaced by justice and mercy"[5] — a veiled plea for his coreligionist. Paquet then delivered an hour-and-a-half harangue at the jury in an intimidating tone. "Control of a grand jury is complete, and neither the grand jury nor the prosecutor can seek review by another court," Leland quotes Paquet as stating.[6] He ruled that "they could consider only those matters brought to their attention by the superior court, the district attorney or their own personal knowledge"[7] and specifically that *they could not subpoena for questioning anyone who had testified at the inquest.* These were unconscionable and surely illegal restrictions (if appealed) on the grand jury's power of investigation. But the Supreme Judicial Court, in its decision setting out the inquest procedures, had given Paquet the needed language for such a draconian limitation on the power of a grand jury.

Leland then requested that the grand jury be allowed to read the transcript of the inquest and Judge Boyle's findings from it, but Paquet denied access, citing the Supreme Judicial Court's conditions of impoundment. Recall that its 225-word conditions of impoundment made no mention of grand jury access, though clearly the very purpose of a grand jury gave it such a right. By this omission, certainly intentional, the Supreme Judicial Court gave Paquet the latitude, or the loophole, he needed to deny access. In their book, the Tedrows sarcastically, but accurately, characterize Paquet's ruling: "In other words, the Inquest record of proceedings was not to be used until it was no longer of any use."[8] Paquet's ruling most certainly would not have withstood an appeal, but Dinis did not want to appeal. He was content to see the grand jury proceedings, which could possibly indict Kennedy, be aborted. The last thing Dinis wanted to be doing during both his and Kennedy's reelection campaigns was prosecuting Kennedy. Dinis's assistant, Fernandes, later stated, "If our office had appealed to the court for an advisory opinion, I think it is fair to say the odds were a thousand to one Paquet would have been overruled."[9] Leland has told the author that the jurors had no thoughts of appealing Paquet's rulings when they were issued because the jurors were unfamiliar with their powers and with legal procedures — and felt intimidated as well.

Paquet's rulings and Dinis's inaction totally stymied the grand jury. Frustrated and confused, the jurors decided to proceed to the extent that they could. Unable to subpoena any witnesses who had testified at the inquest, they were able to call only four peripheral witnesses, who could not add anything of substance to the investigation. The angered and discouraged jurors mumbled "cover-up" and "whitewash" among themselves and then resignedly reported to Paquet that they had no presentments. The legal proceedings concerning the Chappaquiddick tragedy had ended.

James Lange, an attorney, concluded in his book with Katherine DeWitt: "Judge Paquet suborned the grand jury process (our heritage since the Magna Carta), mixed church and state, and clearly subverted justice."[10] And Dinis cooperated passively in that subversion, putting his personal political interests above his public duty.

Among the ways that impoundment of the inquest proceedings could end, as laid down by the Supreme Judicial Court, was "if it shall appear that an indictment has been sought and not returned." The grand jury's proceedings ending in no presentment met this condition. Thus, release of the inquest testimony and Judge Boyle's report could then occur and would guarantee, by the Supreme Judicial Court's decision, that there could never be any further legal action against Kennedy concerning Mary Jo's death. So it was in Kennedy's interest to have the inquest proceedings released. Consequently Hanify, Kennedy's lead attorney, petitioned for its release, which occurred on April 29, 1970, with an eager press awaiting.

A public clamor arose once again when it became known that Judge Boyle found that Kennedy's testimony was not truthful and his negligence in driving the car had contributed to Mary Jo's death, and yet Boyle had not recommended that Kennedy be indicted for involuntary manslaughter. And Dinis had failed in not seeking an indictment based on Boyle's findings. This was in spite of Dinis's thinking, which he later revealed: "There's no question in my mind the grand jury would have indicted Ted Kennedy for involuntary manslaughter if I had given them the case."[11]

With the legal proceedings ended, Kennedy had avoided the most serious charges and his cover-up had been successful, thanks to aid at every level of investigatory, prosecutorial, and judicial action. But doubts, questioning, and disillusionment leading to recrimination, anger, and disgust over the handling of the Chappaquiddick tragedy have rightfully continued to the present day. Chappaquiddick will forever remain an indelible stain on both Kennedy's character and on Massachusetts justice.

A *New York Times* editorial commented, "'The case is closed,' says Dukes County District Attorney. So it is in a legal sense; but it is not resolved."[12] The result has been a shelf-full of books, including this one, written about the Chappaquiddick tragedy, its cover-up, and its legal irresolution. My hope is that this book will bring understanding and closure to the episode.

Chapter 10

Final Thoughts

In spite of the shelf-full of books published on the Chappaquiddick incident, no book before this has put all the forensic facts together to make sense of the events in conjunction with natural human behavior of the individuals confronted with extremely trying situations. What has led to the wide range of supposed happenings and conspiracies in the other books, given how much Kennedy admitted to, has been the bewilderment over what else he wished to cover up. His story left great room for imagination.

This author, having heard a story of a second passenger being in Kennedy's automobile at the time of the Chappaquiddick accident and finding that no book had explored this possibility, decided to examine all the records from that perspective and found it is the key to a full understanding. I found that the entirety of the records neatly fit with that circumstance, with Kennedy's attempt at hiding it, and with the predicament that hiding it put him in when Mary Jo's body was discovered.

A few elements of the account presented here have circulated as rumors before. Early whisperings[1] had Mary Jo as a third person in Kennedy's car, sleeping off too much to drink and unobserved in the backseat.[2] This story was scoffed at and quickly abandoned, perhaps because of the public's inclination then to believe Kennedy or perhaps because any second passenger had evaded notice. Suspicions that Keough accompanied Kennedy, caused by the presence of her handbag in the wreck, were also voiced early. Given the accident circumstances, neither of these initial suspicions is surprising. What is surprising, though, is that no one thoroughly investigated those clues at the time and *no questioning at the inquest was aimed at exploring them.* Various books, e.g., Lerner's[3] and Lange and DeWitt's,[4] have been dismissive of any account based on those observations. A book by Ladislas Farago said to be based on those observations — but also said to be markedly different from this account (Keough drove the car off the bridge; Kennedy was not in the car) — was scheduled for publication but, curiously, was never released.[5] The present book is thus the first, thorough, book-length analysis of the third-person-in-the-car scenario, thorough enough, in fact, to infer the identity of that third person.

The blogosphere has recently become the domain of Chappaquiddick speculation. One twice-issued, two-page blog asserts that the author received a firsthand account from Kennedy's front-seat companion who survived the wreck and adds that Kennedy drove onto Cemetery Road so that his companion could vomit from her excess drinking.[6] Another short blog suggests that the front-seat companion was an unidentified married woman.[7] A several-page blog by Mary Wentworth contains several elements in common with this account.[8] However, none of these short blogs presents an analysis of the forgotten handbag claim, of Tretter's walk as given in his inquest testimony, or of Keough's revelation in this book's epilogue, and none identify the front-seat companion. In short, none of them offers the essential revelations of this book. Several have thought that Kennedy was expecting his cousin to take the blame for the wreck[9] but have failed to distinguish its relevance only to Kennedy's initially planned alibi, not to his new story concocted after the discovery of Mary Jo's body. In fact, none has understood that the implausibility of Kennedy's story resulted from his having to cover up his first attempt to avoid all connection to the accident.

What is surprising are the apparent reasons why those clues have often been disbelieved and not pursued — both political antipathy and political loyalty, not objective evaluation of evidence. This has affected people on both sides of the political spectrum. Some key elements have at times been attributed to a Republican National Committee "Special Report — 27 Questions" of that era. The source led people on the left to dismiss them out of hand as simply driven by partisan politics. On the other hand, Mary Jo as an unknown third person in the car makes Kennedy actually less culpable[10] in her death than in the new story that he contrived to cover his initial dishonest attempt to avoid all culpability. Thus, some people on the right dismiss such an account as nothing more than a political attempt to place Kennedy in a more favorable light. I have purposely avoided political overtones by deferring this work until after Kennedy's passing. I have treated the Chappaquiddick accident as simply a historical event having national significance — the most famous automobile accident of the twentieth century — that needs a factual resolution.

Besides political bias, another factor hindering cool, evenhanded evaluation of what happened is the near-universal, and justified, conclusion that a cover-up occurred. The whole set of facts and claims known to the public simply did not pass the test of common sense. But given what Kennedy had admitted to, what else had he done that required a cover-up? That was the burning question, and there was no consensus on an answer to it. This unleashed in some authors unbridled conspiratorial thinking and political animus that so lacks factual support as not to be worthy of refutation here. A few of the resulting published Chappaquiddick scenarios are simply bizarre.

As a short review of the case presented in this book, let us briefly list those key facts and situations that must be and are explained here through natural — though often dishonest but self-serving — human behavior:

• Kennedy's reputation for heavy drinking and womanizing makes his attempt at a late-night tryst after a raucous party believable. His companion would naturally have sat in the front passenger seat.

• Mary Jo's body was found in the backseat of Kennedy's overturned, submerged car, not in the front passenger seat where Kennedy testified she sat.

• The dynamics of the crash — the car's rotation in the air, its bouncing off the water, and the in-rushing water forming an initial air pocket in the rear seat — support Mary Jo's rear-seat location prior to the crash.

- Mary Jo received no injuries in the crash expected for a front-seat passenger (or a rear-seat, seated passenger). She had to have been lying down in the backseat.

- Tests on Mary Jo's body revealed she had consumed several alcoholic drinks within her last hour of life, far more than she was used to drinking.

- Leaving the party, lying down unnoticed in the backseat of Kennedy's commodious Olds 88, and sleeping was a reasonable way for Mary Jo to handle her overdrinking.

- With the minimal outdoor lighting, the moonless time of night, and the likely reduced perceptions of Kennedy and his front-seat companion, it is understandable that they did not notice Mary Jo sleeping in the rear seat.

- Deputy Look observed a man driving, a woman in the front seat, and possibly another woman in the rear seat of the automobile shortly before the accident.

- Look's timing of the accident is supported by Kennedy's own experiences with the tides in both Poucha Pond and the Edgartown harbor channel and by LaRosa and the Lyons sisters' timing of the walk on which they encountered both the passing Kennedy car and then Look's car stopping.

- Kennedy's roaring away from Look is reminiscent of his behavior in fleeing from a policeman for a vehicular infraction while attending law school in Virginia.

- Kennedy's driving off the Dike Bridge (over which he had been driven twice that day) at around forty miles per hour without any attempt to turn onto it implies substantial inebriation.

- Kennedy escaped the submerged, overturned car through the driver's window, as he related to his personal physician. His front-seat companion must have exited through a window also.

- Kennedy (and his front-seat companion) left the scene of the crash calmly, as if *only* a wrecked car were the result, rather than frantically pounding on the doors of the two nearby lighted cottages as they would have if they had known of Mary Jo's presence in the submerged car.

• Given Kennedy's previous behavior (fleeing police after a traffic infraction), his position (a senator up for reelection the following year), and attitude (of privilege, instilled by his father), it is believable that he would seek to avoid all responsibility for the accident.

• Kennedy's fleeing surreptitiously to Edgartown late that night demonstrates that he was setting up an alibi and attempting to avoid all connection with, and accountability for, the accident.

• Kennedy's fleeing to Edgartown implies he had made arrangements, or at a minimum thought he had made arrangements, for someone else to take responsibility for the then-believed simple, one-car, unobserved, no-significant-injury auto accident.

• Kennedy's calm, relaxed behavior early the next morning in Edgartown shows that he still believed his accident was just a simple car crash, not one that took the life of a friend, and that the accident was "taken care of."

• The long, close, but unequal relationship of Kennedy with his cousin Gargan suggests that Kennedy expected him to take full responsibility for the simple auto accident, as they initially thought it to be.

• Gargan and Markham could not have acted in such a calm, detached manner late that night at the cottage if they knew then that Mary Jo had perished.

• The demeanors of Gargan and Markham early the next morning, as compared to the previous night, show that they had just learned, apparently by diving at the scene, of Mary Jo's body in the car,.

• Kennedy's abrupt change of demeanor, from calm, relaxed, and affable to grim, tense, and worried, after the arrival of Gargan and Markham on the deck outside Kennedy's room the following morning suggests that he learned of Mary Jo's death only then.

• It took Kennedy the next three hours to realize that there was no way out, other than his taking responsibility for the automobile accident.

• Kennedy, trapped by his dishonest attempt to avoid all accountability, could not then tell the truth about what had happened.

• To save his political career, he fabricated a new story to cover up his initial dishonest alibi attempt as well as his attempt at a late-night tryst. A coherent story just wasn't possible; a cover-up became necessary.

Let us summarize briefly how this account has found who Kennedy's front-seat companion was. Any suspicion that a second passenger was with Kennedy was avoided when she was not reported as returning to the cottage with him following the wreck. A close reading of Tretter's inquest testimony offers the answer. Tretter went for a walk toward the ferry after Kennedy had left in his Olds 88 but while Gargan and Markham were still at the cottage. During the walk, Tretter saw the white Valiant (which we know from other testimony was carrying Kennedy, Gargan, and Markham) pass, heading in the direction of the ferry. Thus, during his walk on Chappaquiddick Road, Tretter had to have encountered Kennedy and his front-seat companion, sopping wet but with no significant injuries, walking back to the cottage — a testimony-determined encounter but one left totally unrealized and unexplored at the inquest and, more curiously, ever since. Further, Tretter's four-times-repeated wording indicates he left the cottage for his walk *alone*. Yet both he and Keough testified that she walked with him until around 2:00 A.M. This points to Keough joining him for the walk at the time of his encounter with Kennedy. This line of reasoning thus identifies Keough as Kennedy's front-seat companion. Kennedy, planning at that time to avoid all connection with the accident, would have been pleased to have Keough continue on a long walk with Tretter, so that she would also appear uninvolved with the accident — and uninvolved with him! And by not returning to the cottage with Kennedy, she eluded notice at that critical time.

Other evidence was offered in support of this line of reasoning. Keough's handbag was found in the front-seat compartment of the sunken car. Her explanation that it was left there after a previous ride that evening with Tretter was accepted by Chief Arena, Dinis, and Judge Boyle at the inquest, without any probing questioning or thinking. However, reported observations by a neighbor indicate she did not accompany Tretter on that ride. But even if it is accepted that she did, it has been argued here that any of the young women at the party, *other than Keough*, getting into the car with Kennedy would have recognized the handbag and immediately returned it to its owner (particularly if they were headed back to Edgartown for the night, as

Kennedy claimed). Thus, it would have remained there only if Keough were Kennedy's front-seat companion.

It was also pointed out that none of the cookout guests, except Tretter, gave any testimony at the inquest about Keough's movements, appearance, or demeanor that night. And Tretter's testimony can be said to be certain only on the fact that they had a walk together, not that she began his walk with him.

When speaking to the press following the accident, Newburgh apparently felt that Keough needed an alibi and so furnished one. It was in striking contrast with what Keough later testified to at the inquest.

The last piece of evidence about Keough's role is her own knowing description of the accident a year later, which is presented in the epilogue as a final exclamation point to this account.

Identifying the third person in the car as Rosemary Keough is not an "unmasking of the culprit." She did nothing illegal whatsoever that night. And at the time of the inquest, she simply was so little suspected of significant involvement that the questioning of her was perfunctory, unrevealing, and of little consequence. Getting in a car late at night with Ted Kennedy when he was loaded (and perhaps she too) may have been unwise, but Rosemary was known as a person in full command of herself.

Tretter, also, did nothing illegal or even wrong that night. And it can be said that his inquest testimony was as open and forthright as any given.

What has this analysis revealed about Gargan? He, of course, was a central figure in the whole Chappaquiddick affair. He knows more than he has cared to reveal, though after breaking with Kennedy decades after the accident, he was willing to partially open up in interviews for Damore's book. The evidence presented in this account has suggested, as several others have also, that Gargan agreed to take responsibility for the accident only when it was initially thought to be unobserved and without injury, but we have no direct proof or admission of such an agreement. The indirect evidence is that Kennedy's fleeing to Edgartown proves that he was trying to disassociate himself from the accident and, thus, that he believed that someone else would admit to being the driver of his car when it went off Dike Bridge. If Kennedy's belief was correct, it seems that Gargan was by far the most likely person to agree to such a role, based on their long and close family relationship and friendship. Both the columnist Jack Anderson and the *Boston Globe* Spotlight Team claimed that confidential sources gave them just such information.

Searching out all the details of the Chappaquiddick saga while writing this account has been on one level a disheartening experience. To observe the repeated — almost countless — failures of the police, the prosecutors, and the judges in this case lessens one's confidence in our justice system's competence, impartiality, and fairness.

It can be said without qualification that Kennedy was successful in subverting the Massachusetts justice system, through a combination of inept authorities, receiving deferential law enforcement, lying, and exerting implicit, or perhaps covert, political influence. There was a concerted effort by politically motivated individuals to protect Kennedy. Justice for a wealthy and powerful senator was shown to be different from that for the common man.

However, the irony of this account, mentioned earlier, is that Kennedy's dishonest new story put him in more danger of an involuntary manslaughter charge than the real happenings did. While his negligence in driving off Dike Bridge was still the obvious cause of Mary Jo's death, his lack of knowledge of her presence was a very extenuating, if not a fully exculpatory, circumstance, making an involuntary manslaughter charge inappropriate. Even the charge of leaving the scene of an accident where bodily injury occurred, to which he pled guilty in the legal maneuvering, was only justified based on his false story, not on the reality of events. *Odd as it may seem, all of the mind-numbing ineptness of the police investigation and all of the politically driven laxness of the prosecution and all of the judicial favoritism ended, in this author's opinion, with a proper level of punishment for Ted Kennedy!* His sin was repeatedly lying, not callously abandoning a friend to drown.

Kennedy survived the Chappaquiddick tragedy and controversy to be elected to six more senatorial terms by a Massachusetts electorate that found a member of the admired Kennedy clan, who espoused their liberal, Democratic agenda, irresistible. His womanizing, intemperance, and willingness to lie to escape from his misdeeds were secondary to a majority of them, when compared with his effective championing of popular causes in the U.S. Senate. The national electorate, however, with a greater emphasis on personal morality, a wider range of political loyalties, and a lasting memory of a cover-up, was much less forgiving of such character faults and behavior. Kennedy's attempt to obtain the Democratic nomination for president in 1980 fell flat, with the consensus being that the Chappaquiddick incident had damaged his reputation decisively and irreparably. Most believed that Kennedy had managed a massive cover-up of criminal or at least dishonest actions. Those who believed his Chappaquiddick story had to contend with Kennedy's own characterization of his behavior as "irrational and indefensible and inexcusable and inexplicable."[11] At the height of the Cold War, did anyone want a president who, under great stress, behaved that way for nine hours?

The focus on the culpability of a prominent U.S. senator in the death of Mary Jo has always diverted attention from the real tragedy: the snuffing out of a young and promising life. The suffering of Gwen and Joe Kopechne at the loss of their only child has also been sidelined. Kennedy, in a shocking bit of callousness, totally ignored their feelings in his television speech to concentrate on his own regrets and remorse. The Kopechnes were nice, honest, and trusting people, but they were also naive, unassertive, and overwhelmed by the situation. Rather than racing to Martha's Vineyard at the news of their daughter's death to search out answers (it was six years before they did that), they were passive, ill-informed, distant observers content with Kennedy paying to ship the body to Pennsylvania and, in the process, being manipulated by Dun Gifford in those critical first few days. The Kopechnes also accepted a $90,923 payment from Kennedy, surreptitiously passed through the insurance company, in addition to the maximum $50,000 insurance payment from Kennedy's policy, as adequate compensation.[12] This presumably was part of an agreement precluding any further legal claim against Kennedy. Had they chosen to sue Kennedy for wrongful death in a civil case, where the proof of wrongdoing is lower than in a criminal trial, the Kopechnes might well have received much more money, and more importantly, if it had gone to trial, it could have revealed answers to their, and the public's, many questions. Their failure to do so lost the last chance to reveal in a public forum the events described herein. My hope is that this treatment will suffice instead.

Epilogue

A Revealing Remembrance

Let us close with the most revealing remark ever made by one of those who apparently knew what really happened on that fateful night. Rosemary Keough, when she visited Mary Jo's grave with a basket of flowers on the first anniversary of the tragedy, stated, "My friend Mary Jo just happened to be in the wrong car at the wrong time with the wrong people."[1] *People?* Yes, *people,* a plural noun! In a single word, she confirmed the essence of events as described in this account and which she had not revealed elsewhere. Mary Jo was in the Kennedy car with *people:* Kennedy and his front-seat female companion, who has been identified from evidence in this account as Rosemary Keough herself. But Keough's statement reveals still more. Mary Jo "just *happened* to be in the wrong car at the wrong time with the wrong people." That clearly states chance, not intention: Keough *knew* that Mary Jo did not intend to be a passenger in Kennedy's car, did not intend to take a ride at that time, and did not intend to go to East Beach. For the *Boston Globe's* fifth-anniversary review of the Chappaquiddick tragedy, Keough agreed to be interviewed, then decided against it, but still repeated the above-quoted statement word for word, while refusing to elaborate on it.[2] Thus, its content was revealed not inadvertently but intentionally, and so it is reasonable to conclude that *Keough wished to confirm that Mary Jo was an unwilling, unintended, and unobserved passenger who happened to be sleeping off too much to drink in the rear seat when Kennedy's car plunged into Poucha Pond!*

Keough is the only one of the boiler-room gals who has continued to feel a desire or need to speak out on the Chappaquiddick incident, as evidenced by her interview on the *Investigative Reports: Chappaquiddick* program. In her concluding remarks there, she seemed to deny that there were "people" with Mary Jo in the Kennedy car, meanderingly stating that Kennedy was the only one with her and "that whatever happened happened innocently in terms of people's intentions."

I concur with the absence of ill intentions in Mary Jo's death, but I'll leave it to the reader to judge whether Keough's earlier repeated statement of *people* in the car, or this later denial of it, is more believable.

Notes

Chapter 1
1. Interview of Joseph A. Gargan by Leo Damore, Jun. 22, 1983, in Leo Damore, *Senatorial Privilege: The Chappaquiddick Cover-Up* (New York: Dell, 1988), 74.
2. Foster Silva, statement to Edgartown Police, Jul. 23, 1969.
3. *Manchester Union Leader*, Jul. 22, 1969.
4. Jack Olsen, *The Bridge at Chappaquiddick* (Boston: Little, Brown, 1970), 92.
5. *New York Post*, Jul. 23, 1969.

Chapter 2
1. *Washington Post*, Jul. 23, 1969.
2. Interview of Bernie Flynn by Damore, Apr. 11, 1983.
3. Richard L. Tedrow and Thomas L. Tedrow, *Death at Chappaquiddick* (1976; repr., Gretna, LA: Pelican, 1980), 66; Damore, 169-70.
4. *Investigative Reports: Chappaquiddick*, DVD of A&E program.
5. *Boston Globe*, Jul. 24, 1969.
6. Jane Farrell, "Memories of Mary Jo," *Ladies' Home Journal* (Jul. 1989): 108.
7. *The Inquest*, Commonwealth of Massachusetts, Edgartown District Court (New York: EVR Productions, 1970), 30. The testimony, Judge James A. Boyle's report, and the affidavits are printed here in 129 large-format pages; the official transcript runs to 763 pages.

8. Jeff Barnard, "The Night that Has a Hold on History," *Cape Cod Times*, Jul. 14, 1979.

9. *New York Times*, Jul. 27, 1969.

10. *The Inquest*, Ray LaRosa testimony, 19.

11. Damore, 60-63.

12. *Time* (Aug. 5, 1969).

13. Interview of Gargan by Damore, May 20, 1983.

14. Jack Anderson, *New Bedford Standard-Times*, Aug. 8, 1969.

15. *Boston Globe*, Oct. 29, 1974.

16. Interview of Gargan by Damore, Jun. 22, 1983.

17. *The Inquest*, Joseph A. Gargan testimony, 36.

18. Ibid.

19. Anderson, *New Bedford Standard-Times*, Aug. 13, 1969.

20. *Boston Globe*, Oct. 29, 1974.

21. *The Inquest*, Gargan testimony, 31.

22. Ibid., Paul Markham testimony, 42.

23. Thomas J. Reid, a participant in the regatta of that era (personal communication).

24. Interview of Howie Hall by author, Sept. 8, 2011.

25. *The Inquest*, Russell Peachey testimony, 65-66.

26. Olsen, 119.

27. Damore, 86.

28. *The Inquest*, Markham testimony, 47.

29. Max Lerner, *Ted Kennedy and the Kennedy Legend* (New York: St. Martin's Press, 1980), 118.

30. Interview of Marilyn Richards Gilbert by Damore, Sept. 13, 1983.

31. *The Inquest*, Ross Richards testimony about Lieutenant Dunn interview, 39.

32. Ibid., Richards testimony, 39.

33. Marilyn Richards quoted by Bill Kurtis, *Investigative Reports: Chappaquiddick.*

34. Interview of Gargan by Damore, May 20, 1983.

35. Farrell, "Memories of Mary Jo."

36. Ibid.

37. Myrna MacPherson and Sally Quinn, "Mary Jo," *Washington Post*, Jul. 26, 1969.

38. *Boston Globe*, Jul. 20, 1969.

39. Rosemary Keough, *Investigative Reports: Chappaquiddick*.

40. *The Inquest*, Charles C. Tretter testimony, 28.

41. Ibid., 30.

42. Interview of Gargan by Damore with James Smith, Aug. 25, 1983.

Chapter 3

1. Kennedy television speech, Jul. 25, 1969.

2. Interview of Marilyn Richards Gilbert by Damore, Sept. 13, 1983.

3. Wilford Rock, *Investigative Reports: Chappaquiddick*.

4. K. Dun Gifford, *Investigative Reports: Chappaquiddick*.

5. *The Inquest*, Ann Lyons testimony, 110.

6. Interview of Gargan by Damore, May 20, 1983.

7. *The Inquest*, Richard Hewitt testimony, 82.

8. Robert Sherrill, *The Last Kennedy* (New York: Dial Press, 1976), 62.

9. *The Inquest*, Dominick James Arena testimony, 85.

10. Interview of Gargan by Damore, May 20, 1983.

11. *The Inquest*, Arena testimony, 85.

12. Ibid., 86.

13. Sylvia Malm, *Investigative Reports: Chappaquiddick*.

14. *Vineyard Gazette*, Jul. 22, 1969.

15. *The Inquest*, Markham testimony, 47.

16. Ibid., Dr. Robert D. Watt affidavit, 90.

Chapter 4

1. *The Inquest*, John N. Farrar testimony, 81.

2. Interview of John N. Farrar by author, Jun. 15, 2012.

3. John N. Farrar, *New Bedford Standard-Times*, Aug. 1, 1969.

4. Dr. Donald R. Mills, exhumation hearing, 86.

5. David Guay, *Investigative Reports: Chappaquiddick*.

6. Interview of Farrar by author.

7. *The Inquest*, Christopher Look testimony, 74.

8. Ed Corsetti and Bill Duncliffe, "Theory of Mary Jo Tested," *Record American* (Sept. 7, 1969).

Chapter 5

1. *New York Post*, Apr. 15, 1986.

2. *The Inquest*, George W. Kennedy testimony, 72.

3. Interview of Dominick J. Arena by Damore, Mar. 23, 1983.

4. *Vineyard Gazette*, Jul. 22, 1969.

5. Olsen, 169.

6. Walter Steele, *Investigative Reports: Chappaquiddick.*

7. Walter Steele, *Cape Cod Times,* Jul. 14, 1979.

8. Eugene Frieh, *Philadelphia Sunday Bulletin*, Jul. 27, 1969.

9. Dominick J. Arena, Police Report, Jul. 21, 1969.

10. *Vineyard Gazette*, Jul. 29, 1969.

11. Ibid., Jul. 25, 1969.

12. *Boston Globe*, Jul. 25, 1969.

13. Jerry Shaffer with Leslie H. Leland, *Left to Die* (New York: Strategic, 2009), 26.

14. *The Grapevine* (Feb. 13, 1980).

15. Shaffer and Leland, 27.

16. *Medical World News* (Aug. 26, 1969): 10.

17. Shaffer and Leland, 31-33.

18. Transcript of *Commonwealth versus Edward M. Kennedy, New Bedford Standard-Times*, Jul. 27, 1969.

19. Ibid.

20. James E. T. Lange and Katherine DeWitt, Jr., *Chappaquiddick: The Real Story* (New York: St. Martin Press, 1992), 56.

21. Damore, 169-70.

22. Edward M. Kennedy, *True Compass* (New York: Twelve, 2009).

23. Damore, 169.

24. Ibid., 193.

Chapter 6

1. *The Inquest*, Tretter testimony, 29.

2. *Time* (Sept. 5, 1969).

3. *The Inquest*, Maryellen Lyons testimony, 104.

4. *Boston Globe*, Oct. 29, 1974.

5. Interview of Gargan by Damore, Jun. 23, 1982.

6. Ibid., Jun. 22, 1983.

7. Ibid., Feb. 17, 1983.

Chapter 7

1. Walter R. Mears, "Kennedy at Crossroads of Political Career," *Worcester Evening Gazette*, Jul. 25, 1969.

2. Olsen, 249.

3. *New York Times*, Jul. 31, 1969.

4. *Washington Post*, Aug. 1, 1969.

5. *New York Times* (summary of other editorial comment), Jul. 27, 1969.

6. Lerner, 109.

7. Interview of Armand Fernandes by Damore, Jun. 2, 1983.

8. Jean Cole, Ed Corsetti, and Bill Duncliffe, *Record American*, Aug. 30, 1969.

9. *Time* (Sept. 12, 1969).

10. *New York Times*, Sept. 3, 1969.

11. Lange and DeWitt, 186.

12. Ibid., 181.

13. Damore, 355.

14. *Time* (Oct. 31, 1969).

15. Ibid.

16. *Vineyard Gazette*, Oct. 31, 1969.

Chapter 8

1. Interview of Bernie Flynn by Damore, Apr. 19, 1983.

2. Ibid., Apr. 7, 1983.

3. *Boston Globe*, Oct. 28, 1974.

4. Damore, 279.

5. James B. Stewart, *New York Times*, Aug. 6, 2011.

6. Ibid.

7. Interview of Farrar by author, Sept. 5, 2012.

8. Sherrill, 202.

9. *The Inquest*, Judge James A. Boyle's opening statement, 1.

10. Ibid., Edward M. Kennedy testimony, 2.

11. *New York Post*, Jan. 15, 1980.

12. *The Inquest*, Kennedy testimony, 7.

13. *Boston Globe*, Oct. 27, 1974.

14. *The Inquest*, Kennedy testimony, 5.

15. Ibid., 5-6.

16. Robert A. DuBois, *Investigative Reports: Chappaquiddick.*

17. *The Inquest*, Watt affidavit, 90.

18. Ibid., Kennedy testimony, 5.

19. Ibid., 7.

20. *Cape Cod Standard-Times*, Jan. 11, 1970; interview of Stan Moore by Damore, Aug. 23, 1983.

21. *The Inquest*, Kennedy testimony, 12.

22. Ibid., 9.

23. Ibid.

24. Ibid.

25. Olsen, 261.

26. Ibid., 84.

27. Damore, 361.

28. *New York Times*, Mar. 12, 1980.

29. *The Inquest*, A. Robert Malloy testimony, 13.

30. Kenneth Kappel, *Chappaquiddick Revealed: What Really Happened* (New York: Shapolsky, 1989), 230.

31. *The Inquest*, LaRosa testimony, 17.

32. Ibid., Christopher Look testimony, 74, 75.

33. Olsen, 97.

34. *The Inquest*, Look testimony, 74.

35. Ibid., Tretter testimony, 22.

36. Ibid., 21.

37. Ibid., 23.

38. Ibid.

39. Ibid.

40. Ibid., 28.
41. Ibid.
42. Ibid., 24.
43. Sherrill, 202.
44. *The Inquest*, Tretter testimony, 23.
45. Ibid., 25.
46. *Boston Globe*, Oct. 30, 1974.
47. *The Inquest*, Rosemary Keough testimony, 115.
48. Ibid., Tretter testimony, 24.
49. Ibid., 27.
50. Ibid., 29.
51. Ibid.
52. Ibid., 30.
53. Ibid., Markham testimony, 46.
54. Ibid., Gargan testimony, 33.
55. Ibid., Esther Newburgh testimony, 62.
56. Ibid., Gargan testimony, 34.
57. Ibid.
58. Ibid., Markham testimony, 45.
59. Ibid.
60. Ibid., 48.
61. Ibid., John B. Crimmins testimony, 51.
62. Ibid., Newburgh testimony, 57.
63. Ibid., John J. McHugh testimony, 41.
64. Ibid., Crimmins testimony, 54-55.
65. Ibid., Ann Lyons testimony, 110.
66. *New York Times*, Jul. 24, 1969.
67. *The Inquest*, Newburgh testimony, 57.
68. Ibid., 97.
69. Ibid., 59.
70. Ibid., Boyle remark, 61.
71. Ibid., George W. Kennedy testimony, 70.
72. Tedrow and Tedrow, 188.
73. *The Inquest*, Look testimony, 75.
74. Ibid., Eugene Frieh testimony, 76.

75. Ibid., Farrar testimony, 79.

76. Ibid., Boyle's report, 123.

77. Kappel, 200.

78. Interview of Farrar by author, Jul. 27, 2015.

79. Sherrill, 150.

80. *The Inquest*, Farrar testimony, 80.

81. Ibid., Eugene D. Jones affidavit, 94.

82. The distance dropped depends on the phase of the tide, a maximum variation there of about a foot. However, the measurement was made about an hour and a half prior to low tide (interview of Farrar by author, Jun. 15, 2012), while the accident occurred about an hour and a half following low tide. Thus Farrar's measured drop should be quite accurate. Air resistance is a negligible effect. The rotation of the car caused by the right-front wheel dropping off the bridge before the left-front one also has a negligible effect on the center-of-mass calculation.

83. *The Inquest*, Maryellen Lyons testimony, 103.

84. Ibid., 102.

85. Ibid., Ann Lyons testimony, 107.

86. Ibid., 109.

87. Ibid., Keough testimony, 113.

88. Ibid., 114.

89. *The Inquest*, Susan Tannenbaum testimony, 117.

90. Ibid., Boyle's report, 124.

91. Ibid., 125.

92. Ibid., 126.

93. Ibid.

94. "James A. Boyle; Judge at Kopechne Inquest," *Los Angeles Times*, Apr. 25, 1987.

Chapter 9

1. *Vineyard Gazette*, Aug. 1, 1969.

2. Shaffer and Leland, 91.

3. Ibid., 94.

4. Ibid., 95.

5. Ibid., 101.

6. Ibid., 102.

7. "The Kennedys: End of the Affair," *Time* (Apr. 20, 1970).

8. Tedrow and Tedrow, 95.

9. Interview of Fernandes by Damore.

10. Lange and DeWitt, 135.

11. Interview of Edmund Dinis by Damore, Dec. 10, 1981.

12. *New York Times*, Apr. 11, 1970.

Chapter 10

1. *Time*, Aug. 15, 1969.

2. Lange and DeWitt, 77.

3. Lerner, 117.

4. Lange and DeWitt, 79.

5. Ibid.; Lerner, 117.

6. Sally Swift, dailysally.blogspot.com/2006/01/; open.salon.com/blog/sally_swift/2008/12/17/.

7. Carol Bengle Gilbert, voices.yahoo.com/ (2009).

8. Mary Wentworth, opednews.com/articles/ (2009).

9. Jack Anderson, *Washington Post*, Aug. 13, 1969; *Boston Globe*, Oct. 29, 1974; Lange and DeWitt, 80.

10. Tedrow and Tedrow, 167.

11. *Boston Globe*, Oct. 27, 1974.

12. Tedrow and Tedrow, 174-76.

Epilogue

1. Damore, 407.

2. *Boston Globe*, Oct. 30, 1974.

Index

insurance payment to the
Kopechnes, 173
*Investigative Reports:
Chappaquiddick*, 32, 76, 94, 96

Kappel, Kenneth, 126, 145
Katama Bay, 14, 18
Katama Shores Motor Inn, 18-19,
40, 49, 54, 62, 72-73, 117, 133-
34, 136-37, 142, 147
Katsas, George G., 110
Kennedy, George W., 63, 71, 143-
44, 155
Kennedy, Joan, 15, 79, 83
Kennedy, John F., 15, 32, 80, 90
Kennedy, Joseph, 39
Kennedy, Joseph, Jr., 15
Kennedy, Robert F., 13, 15, 32,
44, 52, 80, 88, 94
Kennedy, Rose, 34
Keough, Rosemary, 15, 19, 27-28,
30, 32, 41, 46, 51, 62, 72-73,
114, 120, 128-32, 136, 138, 142,
149-51, 153, 165-66, 170-71,
175-76
Killen, George, 75, 77, 100, 103,
113, 122
Kopechne, Gwen, 43, 79-80, 108,
173
Kopechne, Joseph, 43, 79-80, 173
Kopechne, Mary Jo, 15, 19, 27, 35,
40-44, 46-49, 51-57, 59, 65-69,
72-74, 77, 85, 87-89, 91-92, 94-
95, 97, 103-4, 108, 110, 114-17,
119, 121-23, 127-30, 133, 135-

42, 145, 147-49, 151, 152-55,
157, 159, 162, 165-69, 172-73,
175-76
Kurtis, Bill, 32

Lange, James E. T., 162
LaRosa, Raymond S., 15, 19, 21,
32, 48-49, 54, 93, 127-28, 132,
137, 141, 147-48, 151, 168
leaving the scene, 75, 78, 82, 88,
90, 92, 102, 172
Leland, Leslie H., 80-81, 156-61
Lerner, Max, 42, 100, 106
license plate, Kennedy's, 24, 60
Lodge, George Cabot, 16
Look, Christopher, 23-24, 35, 43,
46, 54, 64, 66-67, 78, 92, 94,
103, 118, 123, 127, 133, 144,
148, 155, 168
Lyons, Ann "Nance," 15, 19, 35,
48-49, 54, 127, 140, 142, 148-49
Lyons, Maryellen, 15, 19, 48-49,
54, 94, 142, 147-48

McCarron, Richard, 78, 80, 84
McCormick, Edward J., Jr., 16
McHugh, John J., 139
McNamara, Robert, 80
Malloy, A. Robert, 124-26
Malm, Sylvia, 26, 59-60, 68, 78,
123, 152
Malm, Sylvia (daughter), 26, 54,
152
manslaughter, 75-76, 78, 82, 104,
121, 124, 154, 156, 162